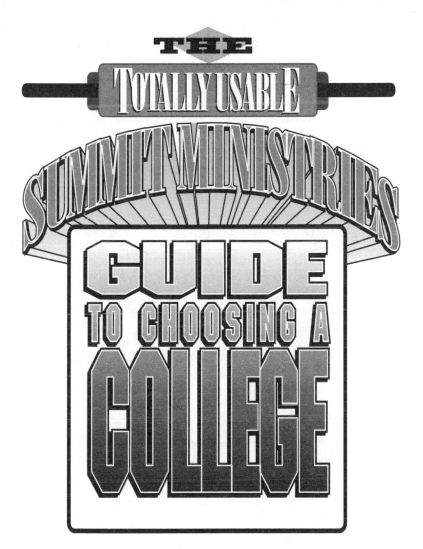

THE TOTALLY USABLE SUMMIT MINISTRIES GUIDE TO CHOOSING A COLLEGE

Dr. Ronald Nash • J.F. Baldwin

PUBLISHED BY
Summit Ministries
Manitou Springs, Colorado

Other Books by Ronald Nash

Is Jesus the Only Savior?
Great Divides: Understanding the Controversies that Come Between Christians
Worldviews in Conflict
Poverty and Wealth: Why Socialism Doesn't Work
Christian Faith and Historical Understanding
Social Justice and the Christian Church
Freedom, Justice and the State
The Closing of the American Heart: What's Really Wrong with America's Schools
The Word of God and the Mind of Man
The Gospel and the Greeks
Beyond Liberation Theology (co-author)
Faith and Reason: Searching for a Rational Faith
The Concept of God
The Light of the Mind: St. Augustine's Theory of Knowledge

Other Books by J.F. Baldwin

Ian: Harvesting After the Fall
Clergy in the Classroom: The Religion of Secular Humanism (co-editor)

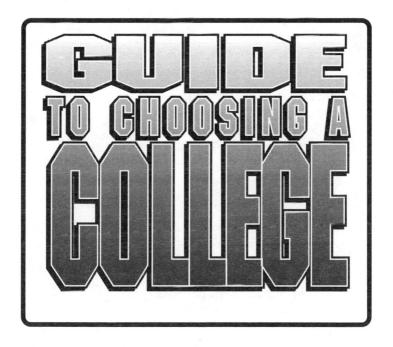

© 1995 by Summit Press and Ronald Nash
P.O. Box 207, Manitoü Springs, CO 80829
(719) 685-9103

First Printing 1995
Library of Congress Catalog Card Number: 95-069057
ISBN 0-936163-34-8

Cover Design by Jeff Stoddard

CONTENTS

ONE

IS THIS BOOK NECESSARY?

It's strange, Jeff thought—*here I am at a Christian college* (one of the best, academically, in the nation)*, and I'm enrolled in a class focused on feminism.* One of the books assigned for the course, *The Feminine Mystique*, was written by a leader in the feminist movement. *Never thought this could happen here*, Jeff thought.

Still, it happened—and in ways that Jeff could barely believe. The first day, a biology professor lectured the class. His lecture was based on a string of bizarre examples of androgyny and sexual metamorphoses, all calculated to support his conclusion: there is no physical difference between men and women! Any physical differences the class suggested were quickly refuted by specific examples of males exhibiting female characteristics, or vice versa.

Things did not improve during the second class period. This time, a sociology professor discussed the "truly just society." In a truly just society, he believed, every type of job—construction, nursing, military, etc.—would employ 50% males and 50% females. "Even in the National Football League?" a student asked. "Even in the National Football League," he replied.

The logical thing for Jeff to do, it seemed, was drop the class. Just one problem: the class was required. Officially entitled "Contemporary World Problems," this course was offered just once a year, and this year—Jeff's last—the "Problem" was feminism. Jeff could stay in school another year just to avoid feminism (hoping all the while that next year's topic wasn't worse), or he could grit his teeth and graduate. He chose to graduate.

After all these years, Jeff still grits his teeth when he discusses that experience. He knows now what he wishes he knew then: some "Christian" colleges are Christian in name only. And choosing the college you will attend is one of the most important choices you will ever make.

We have written this book to help Christian teens avoid making the mistakes Jeff made. The decision to attend college, and your college choice, should be informed decisions based on prayer, rather than whimsical guesses based on tradition or the distance from the school to the beach. This book, we believe, will help both students and their parents make these decisions with their eyes open.

The choice of a college is an extremely personal matter. Every family that uses this book is different in important ways. While a particular college might be a good choice for one person, it could be totally wrong for someone else. You can't just feed a lot of information into a computer, punch a button, and then receive the name of the right college. For that reason, we make no attempt to recommend any specific school.

What we have done, however, is suggest a procedure that your particular family—with its unique background, values, and goals—can use in arriving at a decision. The decision is yours. We simply provide information and suggestions that will enhance the chances of your decision being the right one.

Should you trust us? We think so. Dr. Ron Nash was a college professor and administrator for about 30 years. He spent 27 of those years working for a large state university; he also taught philosophy and religion in two Christian liberal arts colleges. Since 1991, he has been professor of philosophy and theology at Reformed Theological Seminary. Ron received his bachelor's degree from a Christian college, his Master of Arts degree from an Ivy League university, and his Doctor of Philosophy degree from Syracuse University. During his many years as both a teacher and an administrator at a state university, he counseled hundreds of students. He has taught over five thousand students during his career, and has, like all teachers, been surprised to see some students with good potential falling by the wayside and other students with only average potential excelling. All told, Ron has lectured at more than sixty colleges and made personal inspections of many others.

Put simply, Ron Nash is an educator. Like many in this business, he cares about the students with whom he works, and he hates to see young people make wrong decisions. He wants to help them get a better education. Obviously, one necessary step in this process is making certain that the first step—the one in which the student chooses his or her college—is the best one for that person.

Jeff Baldwin is the very same Jeff who gritted his teeth through a semester-long tribute to feminism. If experience is indeed the best teacher, Jeff has learned his lesson in spades. In addition, Jeff was the chief researcher and creative editor for David A. Noebel's worldview text, *Understanding the Times.* He has both studied and experienced the many ways a Christian's faith can be challenged on the college campus.

Can you trust us? We think so—but there's only One you can trust completely. The decision to attend college, and the college choice, should be made on one's knees. Christian parents and students have access to the ultimate Authority— the One who ordained all our days (Psalm 139:16). We would do well to consult Him.

This, then, is the most important distinction about our book: it is written by *Christian* authors for *Christian* parents and teens. Christian families have concerns that secular books in this area do not address. They have questions that high school counselors often are not equipped to answer. They need a book that provides competent advice—not just about the usual issues that any family will face, but also about specific issues that affect only Christian families.

College professors claim to be teaching their students truth—the truth about reality, about the way things work. If no absolute truth exists, any professor's version of the truth is just as good as any other's (and so which college you choose is simply a matter of taste). But the Christian realizes that absolute truth does exist, and colleges may be more or less "in line" with that truth. For the Christian, truth matters. And so choosing the school that will teach you truth matters.

To aid in that choice, this book outlines a procedure families can use to move from phase one: having no idea what colleges to consider—through phase two: developing a list of schools to be actively considered—to phase three: putting one college at the top of the list. We suggest methods for determining which colleges you will want to look into more carefully, and then discuss how to get information you'll need to evaluate and rank these schools. We also outline the advantages and disadvantages of attending a Christian college or a secular university.

The next chapter in the book is intended just for parents. Since it contains no secrets, we have no objection to students reading it—we just wanted to begin by discussing a number of subjects that would be of interest primarily to parents. Our advice to the student reader is to skip the next chapter and move directly to Chapter Three. If it's any consolation, the very last chapter in our book is directed exclusively to the student.

TWO

A CHAPTER JUST
FOR PARENTS

Suppose you won the lottery. Suppose a millionaire found
your name in the phone book and designated you as his sole
heir. Suppose you could wallpaper your home with $100
bills, and still have money to burn. Would you be willing to
take a $75,000 gamble?

More to the point, would you be willing to gamble
$75,000 *and* your son or daughter's future?

Most parents don't have $75,000 to throw around,
nor are they willing to risk their children's future on a bad bet.
Until college. Then, for whatever reason, families will spend
$75,000 (or more!) on an "education" that does their children
more harm than good. Christian parents who wouldn't let
their kids out of the house without a compass and a flare gun
suddenly pay good money to see their kids indoctrinated by
anti-Christian professors.

Let's face it: sending your kids to college is a big
investment, both financially and spiritually. Before making

any decisions, you should set some ground rules and prepare to help your children in any and every way. This chapter establishes the foundation for beginning the college selection process.

Family Differences

Every family using this book is different. Individuals within families vary in their religious commitment; a wife may take her Christianity more seriously than her husband. One or more members of the family may not be Christian.

Families also differ in the extent to which they understand important doctrines of the Christian faith. Some families know the Bible better, understand Christianity better, or have a better grasp of the various conflicts between their culture and the Christian faith. Some families read more widely than others. Some have a longer history of contact with higher education.

In some families, the parents are committed believers, while the child may be lukewarm toward the faith and lack interest in important religious, spiritual, and moral issues. In other families, it is the young person whose commitment to Christ stands out, and it is the parents who may be indifferent toward Christianity. Some parents and young people see college only in terms of how it will contribute to the student's worldly success. In other cases, there is more concern that the student leave college as a committed believer trained to take whatever place God has for him or her in the world.

All these variables pose a challenge for anyone

writing a book on this subject. Ideally, we would like to assume that every parent and student begins the college selection process at the same point: as faithful, practicing Christians who know the Bible well, who are familiar with contemporary challenges to the Christian faith, and who understand the importance of higher education regardless of what kind of vocation is planned, recognizing that the purpose of a college degree is to help the Christian better discharge his or her responsibility to God in life.

If this book ends up in homes where members of the family are not Christians, don't know the Bible or the doctrines of Christianity as well as they should, don't pay attention to what's going on in the world, don't read serious books, ignore the development of their mind as well as their spirit, or care little about putting God and His kingdom first, we hope that some of the things said will encourage them to begin addressing these problems. But this particular book has other issues to discuss.

The Meaning of the Word *Christian*

This book is offered as a guide to Christian parents and students. Because the word *Christian* means so many different things to people, we ought to spend a little time explaining how the term is used in this book.

The word *Christian* is sometimes understood to mean any person born in the United States who is neither an atheist nor a member of some non-Christian sect or religion. Such a broad, indiscriminate use of the term is inconsistent with the New Testament and effectively deprives the word of any significance.

The Christian audience we have in mind is that group of theologically conservative people who have made a personal commitment to Jesus Christ. These people view the Bible as God's inspired revelation and treat it as their basic rule of faith and practice. People like this are often—at least in the United States—called evangelicals.[1] In short, we are writing this book for people who live within the rather large religious family known as American evangelicalism. If estimates can be believed, there are around sixty million such evangelicals in America.

If they are properly informed, all members of the larger evangelical family share a number of core beliefs. For example, they believe in the doctrine of the Trinity. As the Apostles' Creed states, "I believe in God the Father Almighty . . . and in Jesus Christ his only Son our Lord . . . [and] in the Holy Spirit." As one consequence of this, they believe in the deity of Jesus Christ; Jesus Christ was not simply a human being. Nor is it correct to say simply that Jesus was like God. All orthodox Christians affirm that Jesus Christ is God. Evangelical Christians use the word *incarnation* to express their belief that the birth of Jesus Christ marked the entrance of the eternal and divine Son of God into the human race. Orthodox Christians also believe that Jesus entered this world expressly to die. The purpose of His death was to make things right between the Holy God and sinful humans who, because of sin, are separated from God. Jesus' death was neither an accident nor an act of martyrdom. He died as a sacrifice for human sins. It is important, evangelicals insist, that human beings realize that Christ died for us. He took the punishment that we deserve. He died in our place.

Evangelical Christians also believe in the physical resurrection of Christ, the central event of the New Testament. Such people recognize the human need for forgiveness and redemption and stress that the blessings of salvation are possible only because of Jesus' death and resurrection. Evangelicals note the importance that Jesus Himself placed upon conversion when He said: "I tell you the truth, unless you change [are converted] and become like little children, you will never enter the kingdom of heaven" (Matthew 18:3). Christ's redemptive work is the ground, or basis, of human salvation; in order to be saved, human beings must repent of their sins and believe. Accepting Christ as one's Lord and Savior brings about a new birth, a new heart, a new relation to God, and a new power to live (see John 3:3-21; Hebrews 8:10-12; 1 John 3:1-2; and Galatians 2:20). Orthodox Christians also believe the Apostles' Creed when it states that Christ shall come from heaven "to judge the quick [living] and the dead." These are just some of the central, or core, beliefs shared by all knowledgeable evangelical Christians.

This core of evangelical belief is challenged today from many directions—most significantly, in colleges and universities. Professors deny the existence of God and glorify man; they preach selfishness as a virtue and mock belief in moral absolutes; they claim this world is all that exists and that mind, thought, will, and conscience are just illusions; they embrace any myth as truth and deride Christian truth as myth.

Unfortunately, many Christians have such a weak

understanding of their own religion that they are unable to articulate what they believe, let alone explain why they believe it. These Christians are especially susceptible to challenges to their faith by anti-Christian professors and peers.

A Question of Values

You have a choice. Your son or daughter can learn that Dr. Jack Kevorkian is a dangerous man, or they can learn that he is a merciful saint worthy of our imitation. Which do you choose?

In the real world, of course, the choices aren't always that clear-cut. But this scenario illustrates something Christian parents should never forget: families have every right to choose a college that they believe will support values important to them. To knowingly select a college that regularly attacks or undermines such values would be foolish and irresponsible.

Whenever we choose thoughtfully, we rank things according to their importance to us and choose those options that offer us more of the things that matter most to us. Readers not part of the wider Christian family may not share some of the values that should be part of the decision-making process for evangelical parents and students. But such non-Christians ought to appreciate the fact that Christian families have a right to make choices consistent with and supportive of their values. Within a free society, that is their privilege. Within the Christian family, that is their duty. Hence, it is perfectly proper for Christian families to appraise educational institutions in terms of these values.

Some of these values are obviously going to be religious in nature. How could it be otherwise for *Christian* families? Christian parents understandably take their belief system seriously and want their children to share those beliefs.

We have just identified a number of beliefs that should be important to *all* Christians. But some Christians also get excited about less central—or more debatable—issues. That is, they take certain beliefs and practices as important, when others within the larger family of evangelicalism disagree.

Some of these differences are the sorts of things that divide us denominationally. We mention them here because the kinds of things that make some of us Methodists, Baptists, Lutherans, or Presbyterians are also legitimate factors to consider when choosing a college. If certain denominational distinctives are important to your family, then they are something you'll want to consider in the college selection process.

If it is important to your family that your child attend a college related to your denomination, or one which supports beliefs and practices associated with your denomination, it is our contention that this is both your privilege and your right. Again, Christians would be remiss if they ignored their belief system when selecting teachers for their children.

Christians disagree over many things: some of us are Calvinists, while others are Arminians. Some are Pentecostal or charismatic; others are not. Some are dispensationalists;

others are not. When families feel strongly about these matters, they might decide to avoid a college where such a belief is treated unsympathetically. This is not a practice we necessarily recommend; we simply see nothing wrong with it. When a Methodist or Calvinistic or charismatic family finds themselves leaning toward a college that they know will treat their convictions sympathetically, their action is both understandable and proper. Likewise, other families with the same convictions may recognize that these issues are less central than the core of Christian beliefs, and may feel comfortable choosing a college that takes a different stance on such issues. Neither of these attitudes is necessarily wrong.

Christians also disagree on issues that seem less directly related to doctrinal matters, such as social and political beliefs. For example, some churches are pacifist, while others believe the Bible recognizes the possibility of "just" wars. A family that has a low opinion of political conservatism would probably decide against sending their child to Jerry Falwell's Liberty University or to the graduate school at Pat Robertson's CBN University, both of which, incidentally, are fine institutions. On the other hand, a politically conservative Christian family might think twice about sending their child to one of the growing number of evangelical colleges exhibiting a bias toward political liberalism (provided the family knows about this bias). While the conservative bent of Liberty University is common knowledge, the liberal bias at many highly regarded evangelical colleges is seldom mentioned in public. We're not sure why this is so, unless the administrators at these colleges fear it might hurt their student recruitment.

It is perfectly proper, then, for Christian families to take values and beliefs into account when choosing a college. Parents should expect a college to represent their most fundamental values well to their children. Parents must, however, prioritize these values. In college as in life, the ideal situation rarely exists; we must often sacrifice the perfect on the altar of the good. There are some values which we will not compromise at any cost (hopefully, our core Christian beliefs, integrity, etc.), but there are other less important concerns we might willingly sacrifice to see our basic values promoted. An extreme example: suppose you found an affordable college that represents your Christian beliefs perfectly, including your nonessential doctrine, and is an academic powerhouse—but you don't like the school colors. You value the color green, and are disgusted by the colors purple and orange. Must you abandon this college choice? Obviously not.

A more realistic example: you have narrowed your list of possible colleges down to two schools—one affordable Christian college that is true to the Christian core beliefs but doesn't represent certain nonessential doctrinal issues the way you would like, and one expensive Christian college that does both things well. You value providing your student with an education like the one available at the second college, but you also value being a good steward of your money. The decision is not easy. The only way you can make a thoughtful decision is to prioritize your values. As we have said, all of your values matter—when choosing a college, you must decide which values matter most.

Throughout this discussion of foundational issues that parents must consider, one assumption has remained constant: we assume you care about your children. Not a very radical assumption, is it? But parental concern functions on several different levels. Where parents stand on this ladder of concern will affect the quality of their influence on the college selection process.

The Level of Emotional Concern

The first and most basic level of parental concern is emotional. This is where all of us who are parents begin; we regard any parent lacking this level of concern as abnormal. We love our children; we care what happens to them; we want the best for them.

There is nothing wrong with this level of parental concern for one's children. The problem arises when parents' concern for their children fails to go beyond this level. You should love your children. You should also recognize that your concern for them must function on other levels as well.

The Level of Spiritual Concern

When a parent's concern is limited merely to the emotional, that parent's vision of what is most important for the child will be defective in important ways. Many parents seem incapable of seeing beyond the goal of temporal happiness and success for their children. This happiness is usually linked to "a good job" that includes a salary that will permit them to comfortably satisfy most of their material wants and needs. For such parents, a college education is seen simply as a means to such an end.

The wise Christian parent recognizes that there is more to life than this. God calls His children to live their lives for Him and for others. Parents who reach the level of spiritual concern want more than earthly success and material prosperity for their children. They want their children to be faithful believers who love the Lord and His Word, and who sincerely want to do His will. Some of the major issues at the level of spiritual concern are conversion, Christian living, and Christian service.

This does not mean, of course, that every Christian parent hopes their son or daughter will be a missionary. We should thank God for talented young people who decide to prepare for a career in some form of ministry, but we should also thank God for talented and faithful young people who decide to fulfill their Christian vocation as farmers, teachers, businesspeople, and auto mechanics.

The Level of Theological Concern

You will never meet a genuine Christian who disparages the importance of conversion, faith, commitment, sacrifice, Bible study, holy living, and the like. But you can find lots of Christians who have not yet seen the importance of sound doctrine. It is important *that* we believe (spiritual concern), but it is also important *what* we believe (theological concern).

More than eighty years ago, a great Scottish

theologian named James Orr puzzled over Christians who treat the doctrinal element of Christianity as unimportant. "If there is a religion in the world which exalts the office of teaching," he wrote, "it is safe to say that it is the religion of Jesus Christ."[2] While doctrine is unimportant in most pagan religions, Orr continued, "this is precisely where Christianity distinguishes itself from other religions—it does contain doctrine. It comes to men with definite, positive teaching; it claims to be the truth; it bases religion on knowledge, through a knowledge which is only attainable under moral conditions."[3] Orr was amazed that any discerning Christian could be uncertain about the importance of doctrine for Christianity. "A religion based on mere feeling is the vaguest, most unreliable, most unstable of all things. A strong, stable, religious life can be built upon no other ground than that of intelligent conviction. . . . Christianity, therefore, addresses itself to the intelligence as well as to the heart."[4]

Some Christian churches appear to stress *only* doctrine or creeds; they seem to say that the only important thing is believing the correct propositions. In extreme cases, some of these denominations fail to tell people that there is a personal side to the Christian faith. This is a grave error. We must believe the right truths; but we must also believe in the right *person*, Jesus Christ! What we know objectively must be combined with a genuine subjective commitment.

Likewise, there are Christian churches that emphasize only the subjective or inner side of Christian faith, neglecting the objective, theological side. This, too, is a grave error. Whenever this happens, Christians are operating with something less than the full gospel.

Unfortunately, examples of churches that have abandoned sound doctrine abound. One specific denomination comes to mind. Most of its members claim to have had the religious experience called conversion; they have been properly concerned about holy living, prayer, and Christian experience. But for decades, many of the clergy and laypeople in this denomination ignored the importance of sound doctrine. During those years, some unfortunate things took place in the colleges and seminaries of the denomination. In many of these schools, professors and administrators began to move away from essential Christian beliefs; they took positions that undermined the authority of the Bible. Various types of liberalism became entrenched on many of these campuses.

Still, thousands of faithful parents continued to send their children to schools in this denomination. While at these schools, the beliefs of many of these young people were changed dramatically. Many left their denomination's schools with their faith in the Bible and in New Testament Christianity badly weakened. Because the denomination tended to downplay or ignore doctrine, no one, it seemed, paid any attention, while the theological situation in the colleges and seminaries grew even worse. Today, earnest and pious members of that denomination continue to financially support schools that often tear down the very doctrines these Christians would defend with their lives—if only they could rise to the level of theological concern. A similar pattern is being followed in a number of American denominations where the people in the churches are more conservative than those who are running the academic institution. While the faithful church members, who pay the bills, concentrate on their own religious experience, the professors in their denominational colleges and seminaries are tinkering with the theological foundations of the Christian faith.

If your children are to be properly prepared for the years ahead, they should know the objective dimension of their faith; they should understand what they as Christians are supposed to believe. Moreover, they should be introduced to the good and sound reasons *why* Christians believe these truths. The children of most Christian parents enter college with absolutely no preparation for the challenges to their faith that they'll encounter. They have no idea why they believe that God exists or why Jesus is the Son of God or why the miracle of Christ's resurrection occurred. Suddenly, without any warning, they are confronted by a professor who tells them about the problem of evil. Without any guidance or help, some of them naturally begin to think that perhaps there is no reason for the evil that exists in the world; maybe God isn't all-powerful after all; or perhaps God doesn't really exist. Even worse, when and if they ask their parents about these problems, they discover that their parents don't have any answers either. Christian parents who have failed to rise to the level of theological concern cannot possibly be ready to provide help for their children in these situations.

To reach this level of concern, parents must first understand their belief system. Then they must consciously take steps to explain doctrine to their children. This task is every bit as important as finding the money to pay for your children's education. But it remains a job that most Christian parents never even begin.

For parents who want to become theologically concerned, this book can serve as the first step. When you finish reading this you will have a plan for the ongoing preparation of your student for college.

The Level of Intellectual Concern

Now we approach the hardest rung of the ladder to get most Christian parents to climb. With some coaxing, Christian parents can recognize the need to become concerned regarding theology. At least in theology you're dealing with issues that have a clear relevance to Christian faith. But intellectual concern? Most parents' idea of intellectual concern begins and ends with ensuring that their children don't become "nerds."

What makes this last level—the level of intellectual concern—so much tougher to achieve is its apparent irrelevance to typical religious concerns. This level focuses on knowledge for its own sake: the study of history or mathematics or economics or philosophy or art or music, even when no direct relationship to Christianity is apparent.

One of the biggest obstacles in all this is getting Christian parents (and students) to appreciate the importance of their minds. Too often, Christians condense the first and greatest commandment; we are willing to love God with heart, soul, and strength—just as long as we can get our *minds* off the hook (see Matthew 22:37). But this practice of compartmentalizing knowledge into "sacred" and "secular" boxes is unbiblical and leads to the dangerous notion that secular knowledge is somehow unfit for the spiritual Christian. Such an attitude creates the intellectual equivalent of ostriches: Christians with their heads buried, unable to apply their faith to disciplines like economics, law, or philosophy—disciplines that desperately need the true foundation, Jesus Christ.

Although the truth God has revealed in scripture is sufficient for faith and conduct, it is not exhaustive. The truth we can find outside the Bible is also important and worthy of our attention and careful study. We must reject the mistaken belief that faith somehow provides the Christian with a shortcut that eliminates any need for a grounding in so-called secular areas of learning.

During 1987 and 1988, the literary world was shocked to discover that a serious book by a University of Chicago philosopher had become a best-seller. That book, *The Closing of the American Mind* by Allan Bloom, is worthwhile reading for any Christian who aspires to reach the intellectual level of concern. While it is not a religious book, much that Bloom says about higher education will be appreciated by Christian readers. For example, Bloom writes that many modern families "have nothing to give their children in the way of a vision of the world, of high models of action or profound sense of connection with others. . . . The family requires a certain authority and wisdom about the ways of the heavens and of men. The parents must have knowledge of what has happened in the past, and prescriptions for what ought to be, in order to resist the philistinism or the wickedness of the present."[5] In other words, few parents can provide any real help for their children in college unless they also have acquired a foundation in certain important areas.

Bloom continues: "People sup together, play together, travel together, but they do not think together. Hardly any homes have any intellectual life whatsoever, let alone one that informs the vital interests of life."[6] Reflect a bit on all the things your family has done together. When was the last time your family spent time thinking together? Christians need to work at developing a Christian mind; and they should do this in partnership with every other member of their family. Seeking knowledge is an important part of becoming a fully developed Christian (2 Peter 1:5).

Put simply, if parental concern is functioning on all the proper levels, it will include a concern that children develop mentally as well as spiritually. In order for parents to have the same degree of input on the level of ideas as they might have, say, on the emotional and spiritual level, the parents themselves must keep in touch with the contemporary world of ideas.

Most parents are satisfied if they get their child admitted to an acceptable college and find, four years later, that things have worked out well. A smaller number of parents will want to be able to answer their children's questions about theological and intellectual matters, or at least be ready to recommend books that offer answers. A still smaller group of parents will want to be several steps ahead of their kids, anticipating their questions and providing a foundation for future challenges before the questions are even asked. This last group is the most likely to raise godly men and women. How do we know? Because God promises it: "Train a child in the way he should go, and when he is old he will not turn from it" (Proverbs 22:6). The following section provides some suggestions for training godly leaders.

Helping Children Get an Early Start

How does a long-distance runner who wants to win prepare for the race? He trains, and then he sets goals for the race. To be close enough to challenge the leaders at the finish, he must meet certain criteria throughout the race—averaging five-minute miles, say, for the entire course. Likewise, the college student must meet certain goals in order to "finish" (complete his higher education) well. Unfortunately, many college freshmen have fallen way behind in important areas of intellectual development.

For example, many college students are not capable of organizing and writing an articulate essay. Much of the blame for this lies with the poor secondary education they received. But there is another problem: these students simply have not read enough. They cannot spell because they haven't seen most of these words in print; they cannot write because the little they learned about grammar hasn't been reinforced by sufficient reading experience; their paragraphs cannot rise above the mundane because their exposure to the vocabulary and writing style of good authors is so limited.

Bloom believes that students today "have lost the practice of and the taste for reading. They have not learned how to read, nor do they have the expectation of delight or improvement from reading."[7] The rich, wonderful world of great books is as foreign to most modern students as the

American continent was to the pilgrims when they first set foot on this land. They knew something was out there but could only guess as to what it was. The failure to read good books, Bloom continues, "enfeebles the vision and strengthens our most fatal tendency—the belief that the here and now is all there is."[8]

Reading isn't just a drab exercise we endure to obtain knowledge. It's a discipline we can enjoy while growing in wisdom. It sounds corny, but it's true: reading is like taking smart pills. Good readers aren't just well-informed; they have a larger practical vocabulary, they are more culturally literate, and they have an ingrained sense of articulate communication.

The Christian parents' task, then, is obvious: encourage your children to read. As children reach appropriate levels in their development, they should read quality books suitable for young people with their ability. It is even better when at least one parent reads the book at the same time and is able to discuss it with the child.

In addition to the great classics, children should be motivated to do the kind of reading and thinking that will prepare them to develop theologically. C.S. Lewis is a marvelous resource for this kind of thing. Lewis's children's stories are an especially good way to get children to start thinking about theological subjects, as well as getting them interested in Lewis as a writer. Once they acquire a taste for Lewis, they may eventually be ready to pick up some of his non-fiction, including *Mere Christianity*, *Miracles* and *The Problem of Pain*.

Any good reading program must include the Bible.

Make sure a good, readable, modern version of the Bible is available. Help your children to see how important a good background in the Bible is for understanding many literary classics, including *Moby Dick* and *A Tale of Two Cities*.

Reading, however, is not the end-all and cure-all. Parents should explore other avenues for preparing their students for college. Consider working an educational angle into your family travels. For families that can afford it, foreign travel frequently gets young people excited about new areas of study. A carefully planned trip to Great Britain, for example, can do wonders for a student's interest in history or politics. Other students may find themselves drawn to linguistics, or international communications. Parents might also send their students to programs like Summit Ministries Christian Leadership Seminars to help them better understand their worldview.

The point is, start training. Use your imagination. Perhaps you can use the stock market to cultivate a student's interest in math; maybe you can teach philosophy from your local newspaper's editorial page. Just do it! There's no law about *how* you teach your children—it just matters *what* you teach, and how well.

Your child's progress in high school should be carefully monitored. Watch his work in writing courses. Be certain he takes the college preparatory program and skips none of the important courses in English, math, and history. Sometime before your child's junior year in high school, suggest that he or she begin preparing for certain college entrance exams. Most good bookstores carry books that can help students get ready for the SAT and ACT tests. Once you understand these tests yourself, you can explain their importance to your child.

Some parents might object that we are confusing them with their children's teachers. Hear this loud and clear: parents *are* their children's most important teachers. God ordained it that way (Deuteronomy 6:6-7, Ephesians 6:4). Many of the problems of modern civilization have been aggravated by parents' abdication of their rightful role. Christians must lead the restoration of parents to their proper position: teaching.

Besides, if you're not your children's teacher, what are you? A glorified piggy bank? It goes without saying, we assume, that parents can never begin saving too soon to provide financially for their children's college education. But this, thank God, is not your most important role. By design, your biggest task is training your child the way he or she should go.

Don't feel up to it? Don't worry. The rest of this book will provide some of the groundwork and help you establish a plan. More importantly, God will lead you in your efforts to train; remember, He is abundantly gracious, forever willing to use Christian parents who will humble themselves enough to be used.

In other words, there's no need to be anxious. God can work mightily through the weakest vessels. This chapter was not intended to create high blood pressure or tension headaches—we simply needed to define some terms and provide some encouragement. Now that you're motivated, it's time we turned our attention to a really big question: should your student go to college?

THREE

SHOULD YOU GO
TO COLLEGE?

Our time of talking exclusively to parents is over. Whenever we use the word *you* from this point forward, we'll be addressing the students.   Parents are still strongly encouraged to read this book, but they will be reading it, so to speak, over your shoulder.

What they will read here, quite possibly, will scare them.   How dare we suggest that students consider not attending college! Why would we even allow students to entertain such a terrible idea?

"Thou Shalt Go to College"

Why? Because college isn't for everyone. Consider Mark: an 18 year-old high school graduate, he has been working to develop a ministry since he became a teenager. Right now he publishes a magazine with a circulation of more than 5,000, and speaks to Christian audiences all over the country. He recently offered a seminar in a large southern city, and more than 1,200 people attended. Should Mark turn his back on the doors that have opened for him, shut down the presses for his magazine, and go to college just because "everybody's doing it"?

That would be a pretty poor reason to attend college. Mark may decide to get a college education, but the decision must be based on God's will for his life. Yes, there are many good reasons why you should attend college—not the least of which is that college affords students an opportunity to grow in wisdom—but none of these reasons amount to a hill of beans if God has other plans for your life. God may very well want Mark to go to college. But if He does not, Mark would be pretty foolish to go.

No book in the Bible contains the command, "Thou shalt go to college as soon as thou hast received a high school diploma, or the equivalent thereof." It is our conclusion, then, that God does not require every one of His children to attend college.

Clearly, the decision as to whether or not you should attend college should be bathed in prayer. The most important factor in making your decisions is God—does He want you to go to college? Walking in God's will can save you a lot of trouble in life (Psalm 18:30-36).

Another factor that should strongly influence your decision about attending college is your ability. In his capacity as a college professor, Ron has seen far too many students with low high school grades and incredibly weak entrance exam scores that have been "talked into" entering college. These students almost killed themselves graduating from high school; now they find themselves with far more difficult assignments. It's no good advising them to work harder, since they have always worked hard at academics. The only good advice for these students is to pursue careers that do not require college degrees. Many skilled, irreplaceable blue-collar workers never received a college education; nor did they need one. What they needed was someone teaching them the skills to perform the jobs they have now.

But the question before us is, should *you* go to college? Do you have the ability to earn a college degree? Without knowing anything about your high school grades and your SAT/ACT scores, we cannot pass judgment on your academic skills—but we do know that you have one thing going for you: you're reading a book. As incredible as it sounds, if you can read and comprehend this book, you almost certainly are college material.

Is there anything more scientific to go on? Certainly. Your scores on the SAT and/or ACT tests will provide very helpful information. Your high school counselor has been trained in this area; listen carefully to what he says. The advice of counselors (and family and friends), as well as test scores and grades, are all good indicators regarding your academic ability. If these indicators imply that you have the ability, you probably can benefit from a college education.

And are there ever benefits! If you have the ability, and attending college is part of God's plan for your life, a college education can be one of the best opportunities you ever seize. A good college education is beneficial in at least four ways:

First, and most obviously, college allows you to gain knowledge efficiently—to learn! Not only do professors and their assignments challenge you each day to learn more about your world and yourself; your fellow students can spur you on to even greater heights. Education may or may not be exciting in the classroom; it is always exciting in dorm rooms, in late-night discussions among students who care passionately about various disciplines or causes. If you can't get excited about learning in college, you probably don't have a pulse.

A second benefit is closely intertwined with the opportunity to learn: college students don't just learn facts— they also learn what they do well, and what interests them. In college, you discover your aptitudes. Perhaps you haven't taken an art class since the first grade—college gives you another chance to take an art class, this time with an accomplished instructor. If you have a special capacity for art, college is the place to find out, just as with philosophy, biology, industrial engineering, or most every other discipline. Countless students have entered college without the faintest idea what careers interest them, only to leave four years later with a degree and a plan. How can you know what you're supposed to do with your life until you find how God has gifted you? College oftentimes provides the key for unlocking these gifts.

Still another benefit has nothing to do with college courses at all. As the old saying goes, "You learn more at college outside the classroom than in it." College encourages *socialization*, a fancy word for learning to communicate and get along with people. Whether you live in a dorm, off-campus, or at home, you will find yourself interacting with a very diverse group of students almost every day you attend college. Everything you deem important—getting good grades or becoming involved in student leadership or just finding your way around campus—will motivate you to learn to cooperate and dialog with these students. Through trial and error, college students develop the skills that help them get along with people in the "real world" after graduation.

One final benefit merits mentioning: college can stretch a student, teaching him or her to take risks. God does not use us just in our "comfort zones," when we are feeling strong. In fact, God delights in showing His strength in our weaknesses (2 Corinthians 4:6-7). In the "real world," there are plenty of reasons not to take risks—we may have a family dependent upon us, or we may just not want to look foolish. But in college, every student is stretched in some way. You may be a terrific student when it comes to math or science, but don't get too comfortable—your college will require you to take certain English courses. Likewise, you may excel at writing essays, but eventually you'll be confronted with the dreaded oral presentation. Even outside the classroom, a student can take countless different risks: trying out for the school play, writing a letter to the school newspaper, playing intramural sports, etc. Taking these risks can only help you: it allows you to find out more about yourself (and God), and it teaches you that failure isn't disastrous unless it prevents you from trying again. The person who has been "stretched" the most is most available when God wants to use them in a risky or unlikely way.

In many ways, then, college affords the chance of a

lifetime. Grade school and high school provide many of the same opportunities, but only college offers these opportunities in concentrated form. It is not just nostalgia that causes many adults to look back at their college years as the best years of their lives.

Should you go to college? The answer is fairly simple: if you have the academic ability, and unless God is clearly leading you away from college, attending college is one of the best choices you will ever make. This is a hard and fast rule, with only one exception. But that exception merits discussion.

Are You Serious?

While Ron now teaches at Reformed Theological Seminary in Orlando, Florida, he spent 27 years as a professor and department head at a large state university. One fall morning on that university campus, he found himself meeting with a student in her early forties. Her story was simple: "You probably don't remember me," she began. "More than twenty years ago, I was a freshman student in your Introduction to Philosophy class. Early in the semester, I decided to drop out of school and return home. I just wasn't interested in college; perhaps I wasn't ready. Because I didn't care, I didn't even take the trouble to withdraw officially from my classes. So I got an 'F' in your course."

She went on to explain that after dropping out of school, she had married. Now, more than twenty years later, her children had left for college, and she had decided to return for the degree she hadn't been ready to pursue. To clear her record, she needed to earn passing grades in the courses she had previously failed. When asked what grades she was getting this time around, she replied that she was a straight-"A" student.

Did this woman's IQ change in the twenty years between her two attempts to graduate from college? Not likely. Instead, her desire changed. The first time she entered college, she did not understand the significance of the opportunity (and challenges) she faced. The second time she not only understood, she was ready to seize the opportunity and flourish in a college community.

In other words, you may have the academic ability, and you may believe that God intends for you to attend college, but if you don't have the desire to take a college education seriously, you are wasting your time. College is only an opportunity; it guarantees nothing. To benefit from college, students must make the most of the situation. As you already know, great things don't just happen to people who sit around waiting for great things to happen. Great things happen to people who are willing to work hard and open the door every time an opportunity knocks.

Look at it another way. The Bible commands Christians to "take captive every thought" for Christ (2 Corinthians 10:5). At college, students have tremendous opportunities to study various systems of thought, and to learn what it means to have a Christian "worldview"—a whole way of thinking about reality. But if you enter college without the desire to work hard and to benefit from the academic environment, then you will fail to obey God's command to take every thought captive. And, unfortunately, you will find yourself taken captive.

The choice, you see, is not between taking every thought captive for Christ or just "getting by." The choice is between taking captive or being taken captive. In the first part of Colossians 2:8, Paul warns, "See that no one take you captive through vain and deceitful philosophy . . ." He goes on to suggest the only means to avoid this captivity: learn a Christian worldview. View the world through biblical lenses. Trust the Bible as your authority, or be forever bound to the capricious whims of earthly authorities.

What we're saying to you is simple: you are not ready for college if you are not ready to work at choosing a college, and then work hard to take advantage of the opportunities afforded by that college. If you don't have the desire or the maturity to give 100% in both these endeavors, going to college is not just a mistake. It is a conscious decision on your part to be taken captive by vain and deceitful philosophy.

Remember Jeff's story about his feminism class? That story is not an aberration. Countless professors and administrators across the country, in secular colleges and even in many Christian colleges, are eager to attack your Christianity, and to let another worldview (like the New Age movement, or Marxism) take you captive. Even professors without conscious desires to undermine your faith can help move you into captivity. Consider a few examples:

Dave, a student at a state university, sat down in a freshman course the first day and was shocked to hear his professor say, "Let's get something straight right off the bat. Christianity is a myth and Jesus Christ was a bastard. Some of you are going to be upset with me for saying that, and are going to want to discuss it. Don't waste my time. If you don't like what I have to say, drop the course."

Dill Jack, the Colorado Director of the Caleb Campaign, recently lectured a freshman class at a different state university. To illustrate a point about morality, he asked the students if any of them could say for certain that they knew what Adolf Hitler did was wrong. Many of the students raised their hands and indicated that they *believed* Hitler's genocidal policies were wrong, but Bill pointed out to them that it little mattered what they believed, since Hitler obviously believed differently. Could anyone say they *knew* Hitler was wrong? To Bill's amazement, not one of these students was willing to point to the Bible as the authority that condemned Hitler's actions! Students who had barely begun their college education were already captives of a shoddy morality.

One final example, this time at a private university. A Christian student, Timothy, wrote an essay supporting creationism. The professor wrote on the exam, "What you have written is incorrect. Evolution is a fact." The professor then proceeded to single out Timothy in class, referring to him as the student who didn't understand "the difference between science and religion." The professor spent much of the rest of the semester mocking Christianity and, by association, Timothy.

Let there be no doubt in your mind: every college will present challenges to your faith. Even the best school, at some time or another, may assault some facet of the Christian worldview. But this does not mean that all colleges are basically the same; college differences range across a whole spectrum. Some colleges will do almost everything they can to help you develop a Christian worldview, while other colleges are almost exclusively committed to indoctrinating students in a different worldview. Obviously, the Christian student would do well to choose the college that will best support his efforts to take every thought captive for Christ.

Unfortunately, too many students coast into college. They don't believe their college choice is very important, and they think they can get what they need out of college with a half-hearted effort. Neither belief is true. Choosing a college is a serious choice. Attending college is a serious commitment. Neither activity should be entered into lightly.

So ... the final question you must answer before you know whether or not you should go to college is this: are you serious? If college is a lark, or something you're only doing because others want you to do it, you are entering into a battle zone unarmed and without armor. Unless you have the desire and maturity to choose the right college, and then to think through everything you are taught at that college, you will most certainly be taken captive. A recent study indicated that about one-third of college freshmen who profess to be Christians deny their Christianity after graduating from a secular university.[1]

Is your faith so fragile as to be shattered the first time it is challenged? Not if you are prepared and willing to work to discover the truth. But if you are too lazy to engage in the struggle, you will surely be taken prisoner. There is no such thing as "staying neutral" in the battle of worldviews on the college campus (Revelation 3:15-16).

A Risky Option

Do you have the desire to pick the right college and work hard once you're there? If not, don't panic. As we pointed out, some people don't finish college until they are older, when they are prepared to make a serious commitment—and then they flourish. Lacking the desire now does not mean you will always lack the desire. If you have the ability, and believe God is calling you to enroll in college, then perhaps you just need to take some time away from school, to develop the maturity to seize the opportunities afforded by higher education.

Quite a few students take time off between high school and college. There are good reasons and bad reasons for doing this. Some kids just want to prolong their childhood—to travel or goof off before they join the "real world" of college majors, job interviews, and marriage. These teens usually talk about "finding themselves" and "seeing the world," and have no real goals other than avoiding responsibility.

That's a foolish reason to postpone attending college. But other students postpone college for good reasons: they recognize that they are not mature enough to fully benefit from the college experience, and they look at the gap between high school and college as a time to grow in responsibility. These smart ones use the interim to learn—to find out what interests them, and to find out what they need to do to succeed at the collegiate level.

It should be made clear, however, that even the wise student who postpones college is playing with fire. Too many students who decide to "take a year or two off" from school quickly see one year turn to five, and five to twenty, and the chances of ever returning to college growing more and more remote. The "real world" has a way of taking over; college can quickly be crowded out of the picture by good jobs, car payments, marriage, or travel. Even students with the best intentions sometimes fail to return to college, as other commitments entangle them.

The best solution for students lacking the desire to succeed in college, then, is to cultivate that desire as quickly as possible. It's certainly not immoral for you to wait a year or two before entering college—but it is a gamble. Why take the risk? Instead, begin focusing now on developing the maturity you'll need to take college seriously. If you work at it now, while you're still in high school, you'll be mature enough when high school graduation rolls around. That way you won't submit yourself to the temptation of postponing college (which may lead to never even starting your higher education).

How do you learn to take college seriously? Reading this book is an important first step. After reading this, you'll know where to turn for more information about taking every thought captive for Christ. Also, discuss your plans for the future with your parents, your youth pastor, and other committed Christians who want to see you succeed. Allow them to help you develop a vision of God's plan for your life. By taking a few simple steps, you'll be far better prepared to benefit from a college education.[2]

Conclusion

College students benefit from their education in countless different ways, including learning more, discovering their aptitudes, growing in social skills, and taking risks. But college is not for everyone. Going to college may not be part of God's plan for your life; you may not have the abilities to graduate from college.

If you have the ability and are walking in God's will, you should jump at the chance to attend college. Realize, however, that along with opportunities, college also offers challenges—challenges to your faith, and challenges to your resolve. Wise students choose colleges that will be the least antagonistic toward Christianity, and then enter that college committed to work. Without such a commitment, the tide of anti-Christian thought will quickly drag you under.

As you read this book, you'll find a lot of important concepts. If you grasp only one of those concepts, let it be this: choosing a college is a serious decision. Don't paste college names on your wall and close your eyes and throw a dart. Don't choose a college because their tiddly-wink team is nationally ranked. Choose a college because what you learn there will be pleasing to God. And then, when you get there, get your money's worth. Work hard to love God not only with your heart, soul, and strength . . . but also with your *mind*.

FOUR

FIVE QUESTIONS

Still with us? Good. From this point forward we will assume that you recognize the urgent need to choose the right college, so that we can provide you with the proper ammunition to make that choice.

God will honor your hard work. The Apostle Paul tells us that every Christian "will be rewarded according to his own labor" (1 Corinthians 3:8). Though choosing the right college can be difficult, it will be well worth it—in the short run, because a good college education can enable you to take captive every thought for Christ; in the long run, because your work will be pleasing to God.

The work begins here, with five questions. The first four are questions you would ask us—things you need to know before you go to college. The last question is a question you must ask yourself. Not everyone will be able to answer this question; if you can, you will have a head start.

Is Getting Into College Difficult?

The first question is an obvious one: Is getting into college difficult? Naturally, this requires a second question: Are you talking about Harvard University or Pedicure College?

As you well know, there are a number of colleges and universities that are very picky about the students they accept. If you're one of the exceptionally bright people who has a chance to get into one of the top one hundred colleges in the country, *and* you're motivated, *and* God is calling you there, go for it. But if you're not in that league or don't care for the status that many people associate with such schools, there are lots of other colleges that offer an excellent education. Most of these schools would probably love to have you as a student. They will recruit you and woo you, attempting to persuade you that there's no better place on earth for you to pursue your college education.

There are also plenty of American colleges that will admit anyone healthy enough to carry their high school diploma into the admissions office. Many of these schools are reluctant to admit this, of course, so they go through the motions of an admissions process. But as long as they have empty dorm rooms and empty classroom desks, they have what amounts to an open admissions policy. Some regional state universities have a modified open admissions policy, accepting almost any high school graduate from within their state and applying somewhat higher standards to out-of-state applicants.

Is getting into college difficult? In the case of the one hundred or so most exclusive schools in the country, the answer is yes. But beyond them, there are many fine schools that will be thrilled to enroll responsible, committed students.

When Should You Begin Your Search?

Some families start the college selection process too early. If you found yourself enrolled in an exclusive pre-school to ensure admission to an exclusive elementary school to ensure admission to an exclusive prep school to ensure admission to an exclusive college, you can assume that your family started this process too soon. (You can also assume that your family is in desperate need of counselling, but that's another book.) Suffice it to say, choosing a college is a very important decision, but it's not the *only* decision.

It is also possible to begin the college selection process too late. If a student waits until after his or her high school graduation to begin thinking about college, the choices will be severely limited—at least for the first year. If one waits too long, the only option may be a junior college, where the admission process can be completed in a few days.

Probably the best time to begin thinking seriously about college is early in a student's sophomore year in high school. Two factors should be considered that year: you should take the right high school courses (follow your high school's college preparatory program), and you should work hard to excel in those classes.

Your junior year requires the same commitment, and two other steps: take the SAT and/or the ACT tests (described in the next subsection) and begin creating a list of possible colleges (we will lead you step-by-step through this list). The summer before your senior year is a good time to begin collecting college catalogs and possibly visiting a few campuses, although campus visits are best taken when the college is in regular session. Applications should be mailed late in the fall of the senior year, or at least in time to beat the deadline specified in the college catalog. In the case of schools that admit only a small percentage of applicants, an even earlier mailing of admission forms is advisable.

What About the SAT and ACT Tests?

Are the SAT and ACT tests just frivolous exercises designed to waste your time and money? Not at all. Almost every college in the country uses one of these two tests as a factor in evaluating student applications (the college catalog will tell you which one applies in its case). Even if you're unsure about going to college, you should take the tests during your junior year. Begin by taking the PSAT (Preliminary Scholastic Aptitude Test), which helps you prepare for the SAT and also is the first step toward becoming eligible for a National Merit Scholarship.[1]

As its name suggests, the Scholastic Aptitude Test (SAT) measures your potential with regard to college-level work. The American College Test (ACT) is an achievement test that measures what you already know as well as your ability to apply that knowledge. The ACT measures how well you can handle questions in English, mathematics, social studies, and the natural sciences. The SAT provides a measure of your verbal and mathematical competence.

Many books that will help you prepare for these

exams are available at your local bookstore. These books contain sample questions (with answers) that can give you a feel for the test. The practice you'll get from working through such books is well worth your time. You shouldn't take any test without studying—especially a test that will directly affect your chances of being admitted to the college of your choice.

After taking one of these tests, you will receive your test scores and information that will help you and your family interpret them. Perhaps the quickest way to see how you did is to look at the number identifying the percentile into which your scores fall. Suppose your ACT English score places you in the 80th percentile; this means that 80% of the students who took the same test at the same time scored lower than you—only 20% did better.

Information like this can be much more helpful than your high school grades. High schools, even when located in the same city, can vary greatly in quality. A student with an "A" average in courses offered by a relatively weak high school might have earned "C"s had he studied in a school with higher standards and better teachers. Your ACT or SAT percentile shows where you stand relative to all the other students across the nation who took the same test.

No test, however, is perfect. Scores on these tests are not infallible indicators either of what you know or of your potential. In his years as a professor, Ron has seen students flunk out of college after entering school with very promising scores, and he has seen other young people whose scores seemed to predict that they would be only average, excel. While these exams can reveal something about the student's past learning, native intelligence, and ability, they cannot measure such things as motivation, determination, commitment, and willingness to work hard. Don't let the world put you in a box! God uses people according to their obedience, not according to their test scores—according to attitude, not aptitude.

It is always wise to talk to your high school counselor about your test scores. If the scores are marginal and raise questions about your potential for college, a parent's visit with the counselor should certainly be considered. Students whose scores rank near the bottom should be realistic and begin to look for alternatives to a four-year college.

What About the Selection Process?

Colleges rely on much more than your SAT or ACT scores to decide whether or not they will accept you. Each school will take into account several of the following factors when considering applicants:

- high school grades and rank in high school class
- score on the SAT or ACT exam
- difficulty of high school courses
- recommendations
- an application essay (if required)
- results of a personal interview with a college official (if required)
- extracurricular activities

According to the January 26, 1988 issue of *USA Today*, this ordering reflects the importance that colleges attach to each factor; at least, this is what a *USA Today* survey of American colleges revealed. The most important factor was the student's grades. The SAT/ACT scores were a distant second. Of course, the colleges you are considering may assign a different importance to these factors.

Most evangelical Christian colleges take additional factors into account. They will want to know, for example, about the applicant's religious beliefs and commitment. They may ask you for a statement about your conversion experience (if you don't know what this means or doubt that you've had such an experience, this would be a good time to talk to a parent, pastor, or Christian friend about it). Many Christian schools will also want to know about your personal habits. Some of them frown upon such activities as drinking alcoholic beverages or smoking. When this is the case, students are expected to refrain from such activities while enrolled at the school, or at least while on campus. If you disagree with such restrictions and have no intention of complying, you should look elsewhere for a college.

What's Your Major?

That takes care of the four preliminary questions we can answer. Now we must ask a question only you can answer, and unfortunately, it's a tough one: What college major do you think you'll choose?

Kind of unfair, isn't it? You haven't even decided on

a college, and now we're asking you to choose a major!

But we're only asking. If you don't have any idea what subjects interest you or what vocation God is preparing you to begin, we realize it's unfair to make you choose a major before attending college. But if you know what discipline intrigues you, or if you even have a strong suspicion, such knowledge can provide the first clue for solving the "What college is right for me?" mystery.

The reason is simple. Suppose you are fairly certain that God is calling you to be an English teacher. In that case, it wouldn't make much sense for you to decide to attend the Massachusetts Institute of Technology (MIT), which doesn't even offer an English major. On the other hand, if you are convinced that God is calling you to be a mathematician, applying to MIT might be a very wise decision. Knowing your major allows you to rule out certain colleges automatically, and causes other colleges to seem quite attractive. This will help you narrow your choices regarding the college you will ultimately attend.

Some students have "always known" what God wants them to do with their lives; other students wrestle with the question well into middle age. If you haven't been visited by any angels or received a fax from God letting you know what He wants you to do, don't despair. There are several steps you can take to further your search for the right vocation.

Most obviously, pray. God yearns for us to consult Him, and He also yearns to use us—we just need to let Him know we're available. One word of warning: don't promise Him this unless you mean it. If you make yourself available, be available to walk through any door for Him—no matter how scary. Remember, He delights to use us in our weakness. Don't tell God He can use you anyway *except for* this or that; it's an all-or-nothing proposition. You can't slightly submit to God.

Next, get involved in the fields that seem interesting to you. If you suspect that God may be calling you into medicine, volunteer at a local hospital. If writing intrigues you, start visiting a local writers group. If accounting could be up your alley, try to land an internship with a local business. While it's not always true that "you won't know if you like it till you try it," it is true regarding your profession. How will you know if you'll like being a doctor until you see how a hospital works? Working in the same setting as the various professions that interest you gives you a window into that world. What's more, it affords you the opportunity to walk through any door that God may choose to open for you in that setting. Perhaps, after you receive your business degree, the very firm in which you swept floors during high school will offer you a job as an accountant.

Finally, consider taking an aptitude test. Such tests are designed to help a student recognize his talents,[2] perhaps giving him a new perspective on the careers that he should consider. Worthwhile aptitude tests include the Planning Career Goals (PCG) test and the Strong Interest Inventory.[3] Even good aptitude tests like these, however, are not infallible. There's no magic wand that you can wave to determine your profession. The best an aptitude test can hope to accomplish is to open your eyes to gifts that you may not have known you had. Once you see these new options, you must fall back again on steps one and two: lots of prayer, and exploration in the new fields that the aptitude test suggests you might examine.

In other words, don't let the aptitude test do your thinking for you. If your aptitude test says that you would make a terrific forest ranger, but you hate the outdoors, don't resign yourself to a life of torture just because some test said you should like it.

A broader application of this principle is also important: never embrace a certain profession and close your mind to all other possibilities. Most college students change their major at least once during their college career. Even if you have "always known" what God is calling you to do, you may find Him changing the emphasis slightly (causing you to major in journalism rather than creative writing, for example). Dogmatically clinging to one certain profession regardless of circumstances is usually a recipe for disaster. Instead, be flexible enough to allow God to gently lead you in different directions. As human beings, we don't know everything; better to admit it and allow God to change our minds occasionally than to suffer stubbornly in the wrong profession.

Conclusion

Is all this talk about choosing a career making you a little concerned? We hope so. We didn't write this book to throw you into a panic—in fact, we hope to help you avoid panicking and choosing the wrong school—but we did want you to understand the significance of your decisions.

Choosing a college is a very important decision. Choosing the career you will pursue after college (most likely for the rest of your life) is an even bigger decision. Neither should be entered into lightly.

God wants us to take such decisions seriously. In Proverbs 4:7, He tells us, "Though it cost all you have, get understanding." Be willing to work to find out what your major should be, and what career God would have you choose.

In the next chapter, we will help you prepare a list of colleges you would consider attending. Even if you don't know your likely college major, it's time to start making this list. As we work on the list, you can continue to seek God's will regarding your college major—and if you find it, then you have one more factor to help you choose the right school.

FIVE

PREPARING A LIST
OF SCHOOLS

More than 8,000 American colleges and universities offer courses. Unless you are a masochist, you have no desire to study each of these schools in detail. Your time would be better spent determining what you want from your college experience, listing the colleges that meet your criteria, and then evaluating the colleges on this list.

This is the very best way to begin the college selection process. The list can be as long or as short as you like. Perhaps you'll begin with only one school and, as time passes, find more names to add to it. Possibly you'll start with ten or more names and pare it down. Certainly, the names on your list will change. But it is wise to focus your attention on a limited number of colleges in this way.

Some Factors to Consider

Before we begin looking at some of the ways you can learn about various colleges, we need to discuss your basic criteria for adding schools to your list. Does the religious affiliation of your college matter to you? Does its location matter? These are foundational questions that will help you discover which schools you will include on your list of possible colleges.

Religious Considerations

Patrick's first day in his first college philosophy class did not go well. The professor asked if there were any Christians in the class, so Patrick raised his hand. To his horror, the professor pointed at him and said, "Look everyone! Here's one of those people who worships a piece of dead meat hanging on a cross. You, kid, are going to be my target this semester."

Clearly, this professor would not provide much help for students seeking to take every thought captive for Christ. Christians should be skeptical that such a man can impart much wisdom. Likewise, colleges that employ such professors should be viewed with suspicion.

On the other hand, a college that encourages Christian faith ought to be attractive to Christians. The working list of every family using this book should include the name of at least one evangelical Christian college. If a student is going to take courses that touch on issues important to people with Christian values (such as the Bible, Christian doctrine, and other elements of the Christian worldview), there are obvious advantages to studying in an environment that is sympathetic to and supportive of those values.

Another religious consideration that might matter for Christian families is denominational affiliation. Many families have strong feelings about their denomination. It is not surprising that these families find themselves pulled in the direction of a denominational college—such a tendency is completely justifiable (with one important exception: if the denominational college has drifted away from convictions and values the family strongly supports, the denominational college can be the worst school to choose).

For now, however, it makes sense for a Christian family to put a college on their list because it is a well-known Christian college or because it is affiliated with a denomination that they trust.

Location

Geographical location is another factor that can help you add or subtract names on your list. Many families believe it's important for the student to attend a college relatively close to home. This is a reasonable expectation, since proximity to home may allow you to see your family more often, and may cut down on your travel expenses.

Then, too, if the college is located quite close to your home, you may even consider living at home while attending school. The advantages of such an arrangement are obvious: (1) Room and board at residence-colleges continue to rise in cost. (2) Studying at home may prove easier than in a dormitory, where noise and interruptions can hinder concentration. (3) There are important advantages to having easy access to loved ones and familiar surroundings. Living at home eliminates the problem of homesickness.

But living at home also has its disadvantages: (1) The financial savings may be less than you expect. Many commuting students fail to consider all of the extra expenses incurred traveling to and from campus. When calculating expenses, figure how many miles your commute will put on your car and how much this will cost in gas, tires, and repairs. (2) The length of time involved in commuting should also be considered. A ten-minute drive is one thing; a two-hour commute on crowded highways is another. (3) Personal interaction with other students in the kind of close environment afforded by living on campus is an important part of the total college experience. (4) While dormitory life can contain its share of distractions, living at home may only subject the student to different distractions. (5) Living at home can also hinder access to such college facilities as the library and make participating in student activities more difficult.

Two other factors ought to count heavily in any deliberations about commuting to college. The first is the quality of the college. Is the college to which you can commute a school you'd attend if it were as far from home as your other top choices? Don't sacrifice quality for accessibility. The second factor is actual cost. If you live within commuting distance of an expensive private college, where tuition costs alone approach $20,000 a year, it's obviously much cheaper to pick a less expensive school where all costs, including room and board, are less than half this amount.

Remember, too, that proximity to home is not the

only locational issue. Careful attention should be given to the immediate environment of the college. Is it a rural campus? If so, is its distance from the city a problem? If it's an urban school, is it in a part of the city that seems relatively safe from crime? Frankly, a quick glance at many urban campuses ought to be enough to lead most families to consider other options.

Education in Specialized Fields

The last basic criterion you can use to create your initial list of possible colleges is your answer to the dreaded question, "What's your major?" If you know the answer, you will find that some schools are strong in your field of interest, and some are not. Obviously, you only want to consider those schools that can give you a good education within your major.

Remember, however, that most students change their major at least once in college. You could make a big mistake by locking yourself in to a certain college only because it offers the right major. Fortunately for you, there is an easy way to hedge your bets: attend a Christian liberal arts school for the first year of two of your college career, and then transfer to the college that specializes in your field of interest.

To find out if this is feasible for you, carefully study the general education requirements (the courses that every student must pass to graduate) for the university that is strong academically in your field of interest. These requirements usually include one or two courses each in writing, literature, history, psychology, other social sciences, and the natural sciences, and may include a class in philosophy, religion, art, or music. With careful planning, you could spend two years in a Christian liberal arts college, taking general education courses identical to those stipulated in the other university's catalog. At the same time, you can take advantage of some of the Bible and theology courses offered by the Christian college. Then you can transfer to the university that will provide the best education within your major.

Starting out this way has several possible benefits. It gives you the opportunity to take important liberal arts courses where Christian values can be easily challenged, from teachers who (hopefully) share those values. Second, the time you spend at the Christian college may help you discover new interests. You may realize that you're more interested in majoring in one of the traditional liberal arts

HELPFUL COLLEGE DIRECTORIES

American Universities and Colleges, published by American Council on Education, Washington, D.C.
Lovejoy's College Guide by Clarence E. Lovejoy, published by Simon and Schuster.
College Blue Book, published by Macmillan.
The College Handbook, published by the College Entrance Examination Board.
Comparative Guide to American Colleges by James Cass and Max Birnbaum, published by Harper and Row.

(Figure 1)

areas, like history or English, instead of a more narrow, vocationally-oriented field.

Remember, Christ challenges us to take captive every thought for Him. We may occasionally find ourselves in classes hostile to this purpose—but we should never face such a challenge needlessly. If you can create the opportunity to learn from men and women teaching from a Christian perspective, you should go for it—even if it's only for a year or two.

Getting Names for Your List

Now that you've thought about some of the basic criteria you will use in selecting a college, it's time to begin listing schools you will consider. Obviously, if a college doesn't meet your standards regarding religion, location, or your field of interest, you shouldn't put it on your list. If it meets these standards, it's worth including in your initial considerations.

A good place to start searching for colleges worthy of your list is in college and university directories (see Figure 1). Such directories are not indispensable, but they can provide you with basic information about location, size, cost, etc.

Don't buy these directories! Any good library will carry some of them. When you find them in a library, pay attention to the publication dates. If the editions you're consulting are more than three or four years old, the information may be badly outdated.

Another important source of names for your list is people that you know and trust. Ask your pastor and other church employees for recommendations. Ask other

Christian families about the colleges they and their children attended. Talk to people at work. As you talk, remember this key point: schools can change drastically in a short period of time. Schools that may have been quite average academically can improve, while schools that used to deserve their academic reputation can surrender to currents of trendy mediocrity. Colleges that were once quite conservative can turn liberal. Also, keep in mind that the alumni of some colleges see their alma mater through a kind of romantic haze; the school was never really as good as they remember it, nor is it as great as they presently think it is.

In short, don't take the advice and opinions of other people uncritically. Remember that even pastors are not infallible in such matters. We know many who speak well of colleges that have serious problems (these pastors may be unaware of the problems or may not recognize how serious they have become). Nor would we put too much stock in the advice of high school counselors. Unless they work at Christian schools, their values will usually reflect a different set of concerns than the typical Christian family. Many high school administrators and teachers will discourage Christian students from considering Christian colleges.

Another source for names for your list can be found in Christian magazines. Many Christian colleges publish ads in these magazines; most of these ads contain the basic information about college size and location. Be warned, however, that a number of these colleges are not nearly as evangelical as they would like families to believe. In some cases, the colleges are not evangelical at all—they simply hope to attract applicants from evangelical families. It is a serious mistake to believe that every college advertising in evangelical magazines is a school that deserves a place on your list.

Two Books Worth Consulting

We also recommend two other sources for names for your list: *Choosing a College* by Thomas Sowell and *The National Review College Guide* by Charles J. Sykes and Brad Miner. Both books provide powerful critiques of certain colleges—but neither book is explicitly evangelical; each contains some serious shortcomings.

Sowell, an African-American economist whose conservative views frequently upset doctrinaire liberals, has written an especially damning critique of the ethical codes on college campuses. His book is at its best when it catalogs incidents of colleges encouraging sinful behavior and attitudes. For example, Sowell notes that

> On various campuses around the country, virtually nothing promoting the "sexual revolution" is considered too disgusting to be permitted (including pornographic slides at Arizona State, a lecturer at Stanford advocating adults having sex with children, or classroom movies at San Francisco State showing humans having sex with animals), but an anti-abortion poster showing dead fetuses was banned at Oregon State as not showing "good taste."[1]

Sowell warns about the increasing number of professors who no longer teach their subject matter but instead use their courses as a platform for ideological indoctrination. In his words, "One-sided presentations are the rule rather than the exception in some fields or some subjects, such as Marxism, race, feminism, or 'peace studies.'"[2]   Elsewhere, Sowell tells his readers about conservative speakers who have seen their lectures disrupted by rabble-rousing students at such colleges as Harvard University, Northwestern University, Georgetown University, the University of Massachusetts, the University of Wisconsin, and the University of Colorado.

Likewise, *The National Review College Guide* features criticism of much of what is wrong on college campuses today. In a section entitled "The Academic Gulag," the authors identify some of the worst colleges—colleges they condemn because the schools "do a poor job of teaching undergraduates (or they ignore them altogether); they have eviscerated or abandoned their graduation requirements and academic standards; or they have succumbed to attempts to impose an ideological orthodoxy on the intellectual life of the university."[3]

In this section, the authors identify the following schools as havens of left-wing malcontents and social misfits: Amherst College, University of California at Berkeley, Brown University, Dartmouth College, Duke University, Harvard University, the University of Michigan, the University of Pennsylvania, Smith College, Stanford University, Wesleyan University, and Yale University. Tragically, many more colleges could have been included on this list—the schools listed are merely worst-case scenarios.

Is it fair to critique these colleges so harshly? Absolutely. Many colleges provide students with a much better education at a much lower cost. Too many bad colleges get away with incredibly foolish curricula and policies because people have sheepishly decided that these schools are "cutting edge" or "above rebuke."

Both *Choosing a College* and *The National Review College Guide* should be commended for taking aim at many universities that were formerly sacred cows. The problem with both books is not that they are too critical of various colleges and their policies, but rather that they fail to provide proper alternatives for Christians. Because neither book comes from an evangelical perspective, neither book is able to help Christians discover schools that consistently teach according to their worldview. Both books attempt to suggest worthwhile colleges, but many of the colleges commended by these books are liberal theologically, or have no spiritual foundation at all.

Ultimately, these books make the same mistake many parents and pastors make: they recommend schools that appear sympathetic to Christian concerns but have, in reality, abandoned their biblical foundation years ago. Attending such schools can be the worst decision for you, because they lull you into complacency with spiritual mumbo-jumbo, without providing a solid foundation upon which Christian students can build.

That said, we still recommend that you check out both books. Neither may ultimately suggest the right college for you—but both will warn you away from many colleges that are not worthy of your consideration. As you compile your list, take pains to avoid schools that Sowell criticizes, or that appear in "The Academic Gulag."

Conclusion

Now that you have taken these steps, your working list of possible colleges should be fairly lengthy. At this point, you are considering all possible colleges that meet your criteria regarding religious affiliation, location, and your field of interest—at least, all colleges that meet these qualifications and have not been completely rejected by the two books mentioned above.

Don't worry about colleges that appear on your list now that you are skeptical you will attend. As our book progresses, we'll give you many more criteria you can apply to your list. As you apply these criteria, many colleges will just naturally be cut from your list, and certain other schools will gravitate toward the top. For now, err on the side of including too many colleges on your list, rather than cutting a school just because you have a hunch you won't like it. We've got plenty of time to weed out the wrong schools on your list!

SIX

TRIMMING YOUR COLLEGE LIST

Now that you've found some colleges for your list, it's time to begin weeding out the less desirable options. Two sources of information will make this process much easier: college catalogs and campus visits.

Begin, of course, with the college catalogs (you don't have to visit every school on your list!). Once you have used the catalogs to trim your list to a manageable size, you can begin planning trips to various campuses.

Obtaining college catalogs is easy; simply call or write the admissions offices of the schools on your list, and request a catalog and the usual forms for admission, financial aid, dormitory accommodations, etc. A properly-run college will have a copy of its catalog in your mailbox within a week or two. If you have to ask more than once, consider this a mark against the school. Catalogs have become so expensive that some colleges prefer to send other material first— usually flashy brochures full of color photos of the campus, pretty cheerleaders, and good-looking football players. But what you want at this point is not advertising—you want information. Get a catalog!

When the catalog arrives, take the time to study it. The following sections will help you know what you're looking for; when you find that information, write it down. By taking notes, you save yourself a lot of time in the long run—you won't have to constantly refer back to 200-page catalogs that are rarely well-organized.

The History and Purpose of the College

Most catalogs begin with a history of the college. This history is especially important in the case of private liberal arts colleges, many of which began as ministries of particular denominations. How old is the school? Why was it started? More importantly, does the college still take its original mission seriously?

Catalogs will spell out what the college sees as its present mission or purpose. Pay special attention to what church-related or Christian colleges state at this point. Ask yourself if you agree with the school's objectives; if not, you should probably look elsewhere.

Later, when you have the opportunity—perhaps during a visit to the school—try to determine if the present faculty and administration take the catalog's statement of purpose seriously. In the case of many church-related colleges that have turned liberal, the catalogs continue to carry a statement of purpose that may be decades old and that no one connected with the college really supports anymore.

Naturally, secular colleges describe their purpose in broader, more general terms than do Christian liberal arts colleges. The catalog for one university, for example, states that the school "provides areas of study that prepare students for careers in the arts and sciences, education, government service, business, industry, health, agriculture and similar fields. It also offers special professional and pre-professional curricula to prepare students for further professional training or for technical careers." When you think about it, this statement of purpose actually says very little. A thousand other colleges in the country claim to do the same thing. Anyone can say the right words. Make sure that the attitudes and actions of the faculty and administration back up the fine-sounding statements of purpose.

Religious Emphases

Though you won't find information about the school's religious emphasis in catalogs for public or secular colleges, this is something you should examine very carefully in catalogs published by private colleges that claim to have a religious mission. Look to see if the college is officially related to a particular denomination. Is your family comfortable with this denomination? If the college is related to one of the mainline denominations, you will need to exercise special caution; many of these schools have fallen far, far away from their biblical foundation.

If a college purports to be a "Christian" college, it ought to have a statement of faith—that is, a series of propositions that reports what its faculty and administration supposedly believe about God the Father, Jesus Christ, the Holy Spirit, the Bible, salvation, and so on. Be wary of any denominational or allegedly Christian college that doesn't include a statement of faith in its catalog; the absence of one most likely indicates that the school doesn't stand for anything and doesn't expect its teachers to believe anything. Later on—perhaps during your campus visit—try to determine if the college still takes its statement of faith seriously. Many do not. Some allegedly Christian colleges knowingly hire faculty who disagree with the statement of faith; some allegedly Christian colleges knowingly hire faculty who are not Christians.

Study the statement of faith. Do you and your family agree with it? Perhaps there are points you don't understand. If so, ask your pastor or someone who is likely to understand them. Look for possible points of tension with your own understanding of Christianity. For example, so-called Holiness, or Wesleyan, schools take a position on Christian sanctification that differs from that held by many Baptists and Presbyterians. Calvinistic colleges may spell out certain positions that cause problems for families with Methodist leanings. Eschatology (the doctrine of last things) can also be a source of possible tension.

In his youth, Ron came very close to attending a school that not only taught a different view of eschatology than the one he held, but also refused to graduate any student who disagreed with its view. Ron wisely avoided this college, realizing that schools that place such an emphasis on one particular interpretation of a highly complex matter are less than ideal.

Pay attention to anything the statement of faith might say about the beliefs and practices associated with the charismatic movement. This is a very important set of issues for many people; it is an issue that cuts both ways. Non-charismatic families may want nothing to do with a college that encourages students to speak in tongues. Strongly charismatic families may want to avoid a college that views this experience negatively.

As you contemplate these doctrinal issues, bear in mind that many sincere Christians disagree about many of the less central doctrines of Christianity. You don't have to be completely surrounded by people who think exactly like you to have a pleasant and fruitful college experience. In fact, there are strong advantages (at least for certain young people) to studying in an environment where you are a bit different from the others. During Ron's first three years of college, he found himself in strong disagreement with some of his professors. Convinced that they were wrong, he was driven to find answers to their arguments and alternatives to their positions, which forced him to read books that his professors didn't even know existed. Professors need not know all truth to be good professors; on the other hand, it's much easier for the student to find truth in classes taught by men who are, at the least, interested in truth.

Your college choice is a very personal decision. When it comes to doctrinal disagreements among Christians, some of us can live with things that would drive others to distraction. The catalogs of most Christian colleges will tell you what beliefs they feel should be emphasized; study these statements of faith and ask whether you can live with them. If you can't, cross the college off your list. Then find some other school that matches your own beliefs more closely.

Accreditation

A college's accreditation is very important. If a college is not accredited by a regional accrediting association, students may encounter serious difficulties transferring their credits elsewhere. Graduates of non-accredited schools often have trouble getting into graduate school.

There are six regional accrediting associations in the United States: the New England Association of Schools and Colleges, the Middle States Association of Colleges and Secondary Schools, the Southern Association of Colleges and Schools, the North Central Association of Colleges and Schools, the Northwest Association of Colleges and Secondary Schools, and the Western Association of Schools and Colleges. Check to make sure that the college you're investigating holds accreditation from one of these bodies.

All of the better evangelical Christian colleges now have regional accreditation. A few Christian schools, however, hold accreditation from a special organization that accredits only Bible colleges. Some of these schools are places where one can get a reasonably good education, but the lack of regional accreditation is a weakness you may want to examine more closely. Be aware that some schools that are accredited by the American Association of Bible Colleges are candidates for regional accreditation. That means that they have applied for regional accreditation and may receive it in a few years. Keep in mind, as well, that some evangelical schools may be accredited both by the appropriate regional association and also by the American Association of Bible Colleges.

Costs

For now, just jot down the cost of tuition, fees, and room and board at the various colleges you're considering. We'll work our way through the financial maze in the next chapter.

Admission Requirements

Catalogs often stipulate that in order for a student to gain unconditional admission to the college, he or she must have taken certain high school courses, must have maintained a certain grade point average, or must have a certain ranking in the graduating class. This section of the catalog will also state whether the admissions office requires scores on the SAT or ACT exam.

Size

By size, we mean the number of students attending the college. This information is not always in the catalog, but it is important enough to justify searching until you find it. The next best place to look is in one of the college directories listed in Chapter Five.

Some colleges and universities are simply too large. The state university where Ron taught had more than 14,000 students—too many! It is not uncommon for public

universities to have more students than many cities have
citizens; in fact, more than 100 campuses in the U.S. have
student populations that exceed 20,000. Incredibly, Ohio
State University has more than 50,000 students, and the
University of Minnesota more than 60,000! Think about
what it must be like to study on a campus that has this many
students. If you like being lost in a crowd, you'll love a place
like that.

On the other hand, a college can also be too small.
Once a school falls below a certain number of students, it's in
trouble. Certainly, no school has fewer than 500 students by
choice.

Many liberal arts colleges refuse to exceed a certain
size. The Christian college Jeff attended limited its
enrollment to 1,200 students, which was a very good size. A
student body like that is big enough to support all the
college's programs, but is also small enough to allow
everyone to know everyone else. Others may prefer larger
student bodies, but no one should choose to be swamped by
a college population the size of a small country.

General Education Requirements

General education requirements are usually overlooked by
students—until they register for their first courses. Then
these students find that every college has certain courses that
it requires all of its students to take before they can graduate.
In typical schools, these general education requirements will
include about fifteen courses, representing such standard
areas as composition, literature, history, natural science,

social science, philosophy, religion, speech, mathematics, and the fine arts.

The general education core at some Bible colleges and smaller Christian liberal arts colleges is not always as strong as it could be. But this is also true of many secular colleges, for a different reason. Under pressure from radical activists in the student body and the faculty, these colleges have begun to substitute lightweight, trendy courses for the more solid and traditional courses that used to be required. Stanford University, one of the more highly regarded universities in the country, made some regrettable moves in this direction during the 1987-88 academic year. Now Stanford students can take general education courses that are little more than academic jokes.[1]

If you find a college that offers sound general education courses, you can benefit in at least two ways. First, students who do not yet know what major they will choose can use the general education classes to find out what interests them. You have at least three semesters before you have to declare a major. Wise students use those semesters to complete their general education requirements.

Second, if the courses are taught well, they will prove to be some of the most important courses you'll ever take. The best education is a broad education that creates "culturally literate" students. A well-rounded education requires you to learn more than just computer science.

One word of warning for students who major in certain technical areas: some advisors urge freshmen and sophomores in these areas to delay important general education courses until their junior and senior years.

Educationally, this is an outrageous practice. To be blunt, many of these departments are just trying to fill their classes with warm bodies—they couldn't care less about the total educational experience of the student. This ultimately costs the students who decide to change their majors, because in order to earn enough credits to graduate they are forced to extend their time in college by a year or more.

Other Courses

College catalogs list more than just their general education courses—they describe every course currently offered. If you already know what your college major will be, spend some time comparing the major requirements and courses offered by departments in different colleges. This is especially important in the case of students planning to major in religion. A properly balanced religion program will include a healthy number of courses in Bible, theology, and church history. The offerings of religion departments in most secular schools frequently slight these areas.

Areas of Study

Typically, the smallest academic unit in a college is called a department. In many schools, for example, history, political science, sociology, and psychology will each be a separate department. Some colleges, however, lump several of these areas together, so that one finds, for example, a department of history and government at some of these schools. In some smaller colleges, several disciplines are joined into what is called a division. Whatever the unit is called, it will have a leader—a department head or division chair. Should you decide to major or minor in that area, that person is someone you'll get to know quite well. He or she will advise you about courses (or assign someone else as your advisor) and will sign several important forms during your college years.

In the case of a university, the academic units will be grouped into colleges. For example, a university's English department will be in the college of liberal arts, while the accounting department will be in the business college. Separate colleges within a university often have somewhat different requirements that you'll need to understand. For example, many business colleges require that a student maintain a certain grade point average during his first year or two before he can be admitted to one of the programs in the college.

Faculty

Finally, it pays to look at the section of the catalog that contains information about the faculty. What does it tell you about the people who teach in your field of interest? Do they have earned doctorates (even some rock stars have honorary degrees)? Can you tell anything about the universities from which they earned their degrees?

Some weaker Christian colleges can look bad when their faculty listings are compared with those of academically stronger schools. There really isn't much excuse these days for colleges hiring faculty without earned doctorates. Of course, there are some fields where a shortage of qualified teachers with earned doctor's degrees exists: computer science, accounting, business administration, and some other areas. But this shortage does not exist in the humanities and the social sciences.

Visiting the Campus

After processing all this information about the various colleges on your list, you should have weeded out many of the schools you were considering, and the schools that remain on your list should begin to reflect your priorities. In other words, you probably now have a few colleges that seem very attractive, a few more that are beginning to look like distant possibilities, and a few that are barely managing to stay on your list. When this list reaches a manageable number, it's time to start visiting the colleges at the top of your list.

If you're not at this point yet, don't worry. The rest of this book will provide still more clues for narrowing down your list. We'll discuss campus visits now, but you may need to finish reading this book and then refer back to this section when you're finally ready to take the plunge.

Please understand that visiting prospective colleges is not a luxurious extra indulged in by the rich and famous. Some colleges require applicants to visit their campus before they accept the applicant; even if the colleges you like don't have this requirement, however, you need to visit them before you enroll. Would you commit to live in a house for four years without seeing the house? So why commit to live, learn, work and play on a campus you've never seen?

Some things to consider: visit the campuses during a week when school is in session. If possible, try to spend a night in a dormitory—even if your parents are off-campus in a motel. Make sure the dorm life suits you; if you attend that school, you'll have about 900 nights in the dorm ahead of you. Also, eat in the dining room; you may have to eat more than 2,000 meals there during the next four years. Talk to students. What do they think of the college, of the faculty, of the community? What is your impression of the students? Are they pleasant? Do you like them? Are they the kind of people with whom you want to spend four years of your life?

If the college has a chapel service, attend it. Also, arrange in advance to attend one or two classes (including a religion class), and take notes—not only about what is taught, but also about the learning environment in general. Make an appointment to meet the person who will be your department head, should you enroll. Visit the financial aid office and discuss the availability of financial help.

What is your impression of the college's physical plant? Does it look run down? What is your impression of the surrounding community? Is it safe to walk the streets after dark? Are there opportunities for part-time employment off campus? What are the dorm rooms like? How many students are assigned to a room?

Does the school have chapters of such Christian student groups as InterVarsity, the Navigators, or Campus Crusade for Christ? Does it have student organizations that interest you?

When you answer these questions, you will be very close to deciding whether or not the college in question suits you. For this reason, campus visits are integral to the college selection process. We understand that many families can't afford to take three months to embark on a nation-wide tour of colleges. If you can't afford to look at a lot of colleges, fine. Just work extremely hard narrowing down your potential college list and then check out the three colleges that most intrigue you. You may not be able to afford to look at more than three, but you certainly can't afford to look at less than three.

Conclusion

Perhaps your list of potential colleges is still too long to allow you to begin visiting campuses. If this is the case, it's probably because we've avoided discussing the one criterion most likely to keep your parents awake at night: money. For most people, many colleges fall right off their list as soon as they see the price tag—and many less expensive schools begin to look more and more enticing.

This is a reasonable response, but we want to avoid turning it into a knee-jerk reaction. In the next chapter, we'll discuss ways that financial aid can make more expensive educations possible, and we'll help you find the best value for your educational dollar.

SEVEN

GETTING YOUR MONEY'S WORTH

In an ideal world, high school students would wisely select the college they want to attend and enroll immediately. But life is often less than ideal. Many students can't afford to attend the college of their choice.

You've heard the bad news; in fact, your parents probably have it memorized. College costs rose faster than the rate of inflation in the 1980s. In 1992, the average total cost (including tuition, fees, and personal expenses) for one year in a private school was more than $13,300, and the average total cost for a year in public school was more than $5,200.[1]

Credible sources predict that in a few years an undergraduate degree from Stanford University will cost more than $130,000!

Unless you own Fort Knox, these prices can dismay you. Where on earth is a typical family supposed to find tens of thousands of dollars?

Before you panic, it's time you heard the good news. Typical families send their children to good schools all the time. Thanks to financial aid provided by federal and state governments, colleges, and private organizations, students don't have to have a money tree in their backyard to afford a college education.

Need still better news? How about this: in 1992, in America alone, almost 31 *billion* dollars in financial aid was awarded to qualifying students! According to Marguerite J. Dennis, in 1992 "The majority of students enrolled in colleges and universities . . . paid less than $3,000 in tuition costs."[2] The rest was covered by financial aid.

The bottom line? You can afford more than you think, especially if you're willing to work hard to receive financial aid. As noted in the last chapter, you should not strike colleges from your working list just because the price tag is scary. The final price you pay for your education may be much lower than the tuition, fees, etc. you see listed in the college catalog.

Value, not cost, should be a fundamental concern when choosing a college. Because of the abundance of financial aid available in America, you can consider attending even fairly expensive colleges. But you shouldn't attend a school just because it's the most expensive one you can afford. Instead, choose the college that maximizes your return on your investment. The purpose of this chapter (and really, of this entire book) is to help you pick the college that imparts the most wisdom and knowledge for the buck.

Bad Choices

If we told you we knew a surgeon that would take out your appendix, using a spoon and without the aid of anaesthetic, you probably wouldn't care that he only charged fifty dollars. If you were smart, you wouldn't let him perform the operation for free! Some things are *not* a bargain, at any price.

This is true with colleges as well. Many colleges that charge hefty tuition and fees, and many more that seem like bargains, wouldn't be worth attending even if the government was willing to pay you to attend. Before you begin looking for a good value for your educational dollar, you need to realize that there are some really rotten deals out there. As a wise shopper in the college market, you should be aware of the signs that a college is a bad educational value.

The first sign is described eloquently by George Roche in his excellent book, *The Fall of the Ivory Tower*. Roche, who is the President of Hillsdale College, points out that many colleges betray their disinterest in learning by wedging far too many students in classes: "Colleges and universities have increasingly adopted a 'cattle car approach' to education. Classes crammed with 500 to 1,000 students are now commonplace."[3]

Can such classes provide a good return for your educational investment? Imagine: How many times could you ask a question in class? How much opportunity is there for classroom interaction, even student to student? Do you think you'll get a lot of one-on-one time with your professor?

The student-teacher ratio is a useful tool for discovering whether or not colleges care about providing you with a good education. If class sizes average only 13 students, it's a safe bet that those 13 students receive more personal attention than the 1,000 in another college's class.

Another sure sign that a college is or is not committed to providing a good value can be discovered by finding out who teaches the classes. Incredibly, many of the same colleges that cram 1,000 students into the same class don't even provide those students with a professor that teaches every day! Quite a few colleges now rely heavily on teaching assistants (usually graduate students) to teach undergraduates. The average American college professor is in class only 6 to 9 hours a week![4]

According to Roche, "In the last few years, teaching assistants, rather than faculty, have taught 25, 50 or even 75 percent of all introductory classes at schools such as Princeton University, the University of North Carolina, Ohio State University, Stanford University, and the University of California-Berkeley."[5] (Not surprisingly, many of these same schools were listed in *The National Review College Guide*'s "Academic Gulag.")

Still another sign lies in a college's course offerings. Is it possible for students to register for the classes they need to graduate on schedule? Or does it take a miracle to register for the classes you would like for that semester?

Many colleges, including prestigious schools that you can't believe would not give you a good education, close courses almost immediately, even to seniors that need the course for their major. Such a policy can become exceedingly expensive for families: students that could have graduated in four years now stay in school for six. The extra years are not filled with meaningful classes, but with the leftovers that were still open when it was time to register.

"You get what you pay for" may have held true for colleges in the past, but it is certainly untrue today. Some of the most expensive colleges in the country provide some of the worst value in education, because they allow themselves to engage in the shoddy practices listed above. Do not assume that an expensive college would never cheat you in this way. They do it all the time.

Conversely, do not assume that cheaper schools will naturally provide more educational value. Many cheaper schools are cheap because they cannot attract students with their campus, level of scholarship, or extra-curricular activities, so they attract them with their price tag. The rule of thumb is the same for both posh and inexpensive schools: the faculty should be able to provide personal attention to the students, the students should be able to enroll in the classes they want, and the level of scholarship should be commendable. This will not ensure that the college will help you take captive every thought for Christ, but it will ensure that the college is concerned with maximizing the money you spend on education.

Calculating Actual Cost

By applying this "value criterion" you should hopefully have trimmed a few more names from your list of potential colleges. Still, you can't know whether or not some colleges are a good value until you know how much they actually will cost you. It's time, then, to find out what all this is really going to cost.

A college education costs more than just tuition. When figuring how much it will cost to attend a school, factor in all these variables: tuition, fees, books and supplies, room and board, transportation, insurance, and personal expenses. Now brace yourself and look at the total. Gasp, drink a glass of water, and sit down. Remember that your actual cost should be largely defrayed by financial aid.

Financial aid makes every school more affordable. Strangely, it also often makes your actual cost for college roughly the same regardless of the school you choose. Sound crazy? Bear with us a moment.

Suppose, for the sake of argument, that you have four schools left on your list. One is a public university, and the other three are small liberal arts college. Suppose your total cost for one year at the public school is around $6,000, and your total cost for the other colleges ranges from $10,000 to $16,000 per year. Do not automatically assume that it will be cheaper for you to attend the public university! Though it sounds odd, it is quite possible that financial aid will allow you to attend one of the private colleges for the same, or even less, than the public university.

The reason is simple. When colleges or the government evaluate your request for financial aid, they arrive at a figure that represents your Expected Family Contribution (EFC)—the amount of money they expect your family to spend annually on your college education. They subtract this figure from the total cost of your college education to arrive at your "financial need"—the amount of aid you would have to have to afford a particular college. Your EFC does not fluctuate; it remains constant whether you are considering an expensive or inexpensive college.

Instead, it is your financial need that fluctuates. For the most expensive private school on your list you may need $12,000, while you would only need $2,000 to attend the public university. If you apply to the private school, and they are really interested in enrolling you as a student, they will recognize that your financial need merits a financial aid package in the $12,000 range. Offering you just $3,000 would be just like rejecting your application in the first place, because they have already established that your family cannot afford to make up the difference.

Naturally, it helps if the college *really* wants you as a student. But even if the school feels somewhat ambivalent about you, private financial aid institutions or the government might provide enough financial aid to make it possible for you to attend the college.

Though we've said it twice, we'll say it again: don't scratch a school from your working list just because it carries an expensive price tag. It's possible that you might not have to pay anywhere near that price to attend the college. Before scratching any college off your list for monetary reasons, find out the actual cost: the total price tag minus your financial aid package.

The Financial Aid Maze

To find out this information, of course, you must begin to navigate the maze of financial aid forms and options. Almost immediately, you will discover a catch: financial aid packages are usually only offered to students during the year they expect to begin their college education. If you aren't going to attend college for a year or more, no one will be very interested in awarding you financial aid.

This means that you must adhere to a very tight schedule as you work through the financial aid process. By the time January 1 of the year you plan to attend college rolls around, you should have narrowed your list of potential schools to somewhere between one and five. This gives you a manageable number of schools for which you will need to determine the actual cost. Any more schools, and you probably won't be able to meet all the deadlines to qualify for financial aid offers for each of the schools on your list. Without financial aid offers, you don't know how much a school is really going to cost!

Those who had hoped to use the cost factor to weed numerous names from their list of potential colleges have just encountered a harsh reality: you only have time to discover the actual cost for about five colleges. You'll have to rely on other criteria to cut your list down to five schools.

Once you've accomplished that, you're ready to enter the maze. If you follow the steps outlined here, your excursion should be both pain-free and fruitful.

Begin by finding out which standardized need analysis forms your prospective colleges accept. The two most common need analysis forms (that is, the forms that establish your EFC and your financial need) are the Financial Aid Form (FAF) and the Family Financial Statement (FFS). Your high school counselor can provide you with either of these. You will also probably have to fill out a separate financial aid application for every college that you are considering. Request these forms well in advance, realizing that you are not allowed to complete them until after January 1 of the year you plan to enter college.

As soon as January 1 hits, work feverishly to complete these forms (while simultaneously working feverishly to fill out your enrollment applications). Photocopy each form for your records, and then mail them as quickly as possible. After finishing these, begin applying for financial aid from private organizations (we'll recommend books that detail private organizations that offer aid later in the chapter). After you've done all you can do, brace yourself for the wait.

In February, you should receive a confirmation from the need analysis service that processes your FAF or FFS. This confirmation will allow you to verify that the information you submitted to the service has been processed correctly. After verifying this and returning the confirmation, you must wait again.

Around March, you will finally receive a report from the service that informs you of your EFC and your eligibility for financial aid. The colleges you are considering and your state's scholarship agency will receive a similar report at the same time. And then—did you guess?—it's time to wait some more.

Most colleges make their financial aid decisions between March and July (obviously, they'll let you know whether or not they accepted your enrollment application before they offer you financial aid). When they have made their decisions, they will send you a financial aid award letter. This letter will tell you what the college believes to be your EFC and how much aid you have been awarded for that year. The financial aid awarded will include all financial aid provided by the federal or state government, private organizations, and the college itself.

Then and only then will you be able to determine your actual cost for a college. Referring back to the total price tag of the school, subtract the total financial aid awarded from this price. This is your actual cost. You can compare the actual costs of all the colleges still left on your working list. Finally, you should begin to have a clearer picture of the college that provides the best educational value.

As you study the financial aid packages offered by the colleges that interest you, pay attention to the components of the package. Aid usually falls into three basic categories: scholarships, grants, and loans. Not all aid is equal. Scholarships and grants provide "free money" that you will never have to repay (though you may have to maintain academic excellence to receive a scholarship). Loans, on the other hand, must be repaid. These loans are usually low-interest and a pretty good deal, but this does not negate the fact that "free money" is better than borrowed money. Aid packages that are heavy on loans and light on grants are not as attractive as the converse. If you have the choice, the college that offers the package packed with grants and scholarships is offering you the better deal.

Still other factors come into play. If you are unhappy with the financial aid award offered by one or more colleges, you can appeal to each school's director of financial aid. In certain circumstances, this person can exercise "professional judgment" and offer you a different financial aid package. Also, if new circumstances like an extended illness or unemployment negatively impact your family's ability to provide for your education, each school's director of financial aid should be notified immediately.

After all the applications, calculations, and appeals, you should have a pretty good idea of which colleges you can afford. Hopefully, you won't have to cut any of your "finalist" colleges just because of finances. If some of these finalists still look too expensive, however, read on—we haven't yet exhausted the ways to cut college costs.

Working and Studying

As scary as it sounds, many students manage to afford the college of their choice by working part-time or full-time while attending school. Though it seems like too much extra responsibility for a student facing the most challenging courses he's ever faced, the fact remains that many students who work flourish. Studies suggest that college students who work 10 or 20 hours a week experience no negative academic effects.

In fact, students who work usually benefit in at least one way: their job experience can help them make decisions about the careers that interest them, and can even establish the foundation for those careers. Employers will always be more interested in applicants who have both a college degree *and* on-the-job experience.

If you are disciplined enough to shoulder the responsibility of both a job and academic work, then you should certainly consider all employment program options. There are plenty!

The most obvious option, of course, is to find a job on your own. Once you've selected your college, you can check the classified ads, visit local businesses, and generally beat the pavement until you find work you like. This is by far the most difficult, and least efficient, way to earn money for your education.

The best way is to talk with your college's financial aid director and career counselors to discover the employment options offered by the college, the federal and state governments, and private organizations. As you'll discover, there are five major employment programs: federal College Work-Study Programs, state Work-Study Programs, institutional employment programs, company-paid tuition programs, and Cooperative Education programs.

Obviously, the federal and state Work-Study Programs are quite similar. Both options provide employment for students who exhibit financial need, and both are awarded when you receive the rest of your financial aid package. Either you qualify for these programs or you don't. For this reason, we won't dwell on these options.

The institutional employment programs are administered by the schools themselves. These programs are *not* need-based, so that any student seeking employment may apply. The jobs provided are usually on-campus, which makes it convenient for students who don't have their own car. Also, this program affords you the opportunity to interact with even more students than you normally would.

One specialized example of an institutional employment program is the Resident Advisor program. Students who participate in this program live in the dorm, monitoring and helping fellow students in exchange for reduced room and board costs. Both Resident Advisor and Resident Assistant positions give you the chance to develop leadership and team-building skills.

Company-paid tuition programs pay a portion of their employees' college expenses. Sometimes these programs require participating employees to take only job-related classes, and sometimes the employee must commit to work for the company a specific amount of time after graduation. Generally speaking, these programs are more difficult to locate—though college career counselors should be aware of some opportunities.

Perhaps the most appealing major employment program, however, is the Cooperative Education program. Students who participate in this program alternate between studying full-time and working full-time, so that they are able to give their full concentration to both activities. According to this pattern, a student might attend college full-time during the winter term, then work full-time during spring term, then transition back to school for the summer, and continue in this way until graduation. It usually takes a student five years to earn his bachelors degree when he works with this program, but it is well worth it. Students can choose jobs in the fields that interest them, and the program is not based on financial need. Participating in this program can take a huge bite out of your total college costs.[6]

Granted, working while attending college isn't for everyone—it requires initiative and perseverance. If you want to attend a certain college badly enough, however, you may find it worth your while to learn these traits, and to get involved in an employment program.

More Cost-Cutting Options

Now it's time to pull out all the stops. We've surveyed the really significant ways to get the most college education for your money, but there are still other details that will allow you to further cut costs. Though some of these details will represent only modest savings, it's worth mentioning them all. As you have certainly realized by now, when it comes to college every penny counts.

The first factor you may want to consider is that state colleges and universities offer much less expensive tuition for in-state residents than out-of-state students. It has been estimated that families can save up to 40% of the total college bill (before financial aid) by sending their student to local state colleges.

Second, make wise decisions about the books that you buy for your courses. You can save a fair amount of money by purchasing used, rather than new, textbooks. Also, consider splitting the cost of a textbook with a friend in the class. Above all, be certain that you won't drop the course before you invest in the books.

Third, you may be able to save money by reducing the number of credits you need to graduate. Some schools allow you to do this by testing you in certain subject areas; if you demonstrate enough knowledge about the subject, the college will allow you to forego taking an otherwise required course. These tests are usually provided by the College-Level Examination Program (CLEP).

Fourth, some companies help their employees pay college costs for their children. It's obviously well worth your parents' time to find out if their employer offers such a program. It's also worth your time to see if the colleges in which you are interested offer reduced tuition for children of alumni. If your folks went to a certain college, that college might be willing to charge you less.

We also should mention one way that you can save money by *not* taking action. Don't bother spending your money on the services of a scholarship search firm! These firms promise to help you locate scholarships for which you might qualify—which sounds great—but they usually charge between $50-$200 to provide this service. With a little work, you can locate the scholarships that may fit you all by yourself, at no cost. The easiest way to do this is to check out some of the well-written books about college costs and financial aid (see Figure 2). Many of these books provide lists of available scholarships and the corresponding criteria you must fulfill to qualify for the scholarships.

But that's not all they provide. They'll also help you better understand how to get the most education for your money. Don't assume that you know it all just because you've read this chapter! Look at these books, and work

WORTHWHILE BOOKS ABOUT COLLEGE FINANCES

The College Cost Book (New York: College Entrance Exam
    Board, 1992).
College Financial Aid (New York: Arco Publishing, 1991).
Keys to Financing a College Education by Marguerite J.
    Dennis (New York: Barron's, 1993).
Peterson's College Money Handbook ed. by Susan W. Dilts
    (Princeton, NJ: Peterson's, 1992).
The Scholarship Book by Daniel J. Cassidy (Englewood
    Cliffs, NJ: Prentice-Hall, 1993).
The Student Access Guide to Paying for College by Kalman
    A. Chany and Geoff Martz (New York: Villard Books,
    1992).

(Figure 2)

hard to use your money (and your parents' money) wisely.
God expects us to be good stewards (Luke 16:10-11).

Conclusion

Financing a college education can be a scary thing. But it
becomes a lot less scary when you know the best methods to
maximize the return on your educational investment. When
you avoid schools that provide a bad value, when you
successfully navigate the financial aid maze, and when you
use other available cost-cutting options, you take substantial
strides toward getting the most for your money.

If you're still a little nervous, remember that it could
always be worse. Jeff's oldest child won't be in college for

another 17 years, when (according to conservative estimates) the average total cost for one year at a private college will be more than $40,000!

The next chapter will deal specifically with the different types of nonevangelical colleges, and then Chapter Nine will describe evangelical colleges. These chapters will mention some of the colleges that provide a good educational value, and help you develop some realistic expectations about the schools you are considering.

EIGHT

NONEVANGELICAL COLLEGES

By now, you probably have the feeling that we would rather see you attend an evangelical college than a nonevangelical school. You're right! All other factors being equal, an evangelical college that is truly committed to Christ will impart more wisdom than any other school you could attend.

We realize, however, that it is not always possible for young people from Christian families to attend an evangelical college—and so this chapter will look specifically at nonevangelical college options: the public university, the secular private college, and the nonevangelical denominational college. Students without any nonevangelical colleges on their working list may safely skip to Chapter Nine.

The Public University

Most of the public colleges and universities we discuss in this section are state-supported universities. Some public universities, such as the City University of New York, the University of Cincinnati, and the University of Louisville, began largely due to city funding, but the majority of municipal colleges and universities now receive some percentage of their budget from the state government.

In many states there is a rather clear-cut distinction, in terms of financial support and prestige, between the major state university and so-called regional universities. In Illinois, for example, the University of Illinois at Champaign/Urbana gets most of the attention in the state. Illinois' regional universities have such names as Northern Illinois and Southern Illinois. This tendency to identify regional universities exists in many other states including Kentucky (Western Kentucky University and Eastern Kentucky University) and Florida (the University of South Florida and the University of West Florida).

Most major public universities benefit from often-inexplicable fan support for their football and basketball programs. This results in a common kind of irrational behavior in which thousands of high school graduates choose a university primarily because of its athletic teams. These young people know nothing about the academic reputation of these schools; all they know is that they love "the Big Blue" (Kentucky), "the Big Orange" (Tennessee), or "the Big Red" (Nebraska). We cannot imagine a worse way to select a college.

Besides major state universities and regional universities, several states also have large, state-supported technical schools. Examples include Texas Tech, Texas A&M, Georgia Tech, and Virginia Tech. Many southern states also have public colleges that used to be exclusively for black students. While schools like Kentucky State and Tennessee State have taken major strides toward integration, they continue to be primarily black institutions.

State universities are often very big places. Ohio State University in Columbus has about 53,000 students! Ohio's regional universities are big enough in their own right: Bowling Green State University has about 17,000, while Kent State has approximately 20,000 students. The University of Michigan's student enrollment comes in at around 35,000, while Michigan State's tops 42,000.

Schools this size are obviously big enough to offer courses and programs in just about any area that any person might want to study. If the only courses that interest you are those that focus on avian taxidermy, you'll probably have to attend a state university. While no one, either in the administration of these schools or in the state legislatures that provide the tax dollars, ever asks whether all these programs can be justified on academic grounds, the public monies keep pouring in, and the students keep pouring out.

Because of the support they receive from tax dollars, public universities have an enormous and often unfair advantage over private colleges. The public universities can be much cheaper to attend. Private colleges, which often offer a superior education, are forced to charge much higher tuition, thus making it increasingly difficult for them to compete in the race to recruit students.

Most of the Christian families who have settled on a public university as their first choice cite one or two reasons for their choice. The first is money. The significantly lower price tag of a public university often tips the scales. This price tag becomes especially enticing when the public school is also within commuting distance of the family's home. The family then gets the added benefit of eliminating the expense of room and board.

The other reason arises in situations where the student knows (or believes) that he or she is going to specialize in some professional or pre-professional area that may not be offered by the evangelical colleges. There may also be good reason to believe that even if the program is available in a Christian college, the one offered in the larger and better-financed state university is superior. This is often true, for example, in areas like computer science. We have already warned, however, against making too much of this matter. The world often looks quite different to students by the time they reach their second or third year in college. They may discover new interests, or their grades may fall below acceptable limits. It is wise to be flexible and leave yourself other options if things don't work out as you planned. Remember, you can always take your first year or two of general education courses in a fully accredited, Christian liberal arts college and then transfer those credits to the public university where you'll pursue your technical or specialized program.

These reasons for attending a public school are often outweighed by negatives. For one thing, the sheer size of many of these schools ought to make them unappealing. Nothing can bring this home more quickly than a personal visit to one of these small cities. Spend some time walking around the huge campus while the college is in session and ask yourself whether you really want to submerge yourself in this anonymous mass of humanity.

This basic problem implies a second, more serious problem: at big schools, it is impossible to get to know more than a small percentage of the faculty and students. This is a high price to pay. Talk to people who graduated from smaller colleges where they were part of a community. As one book puts it, "the ultimate value of a college education derives not simply from taking classes or passing exams but from the ongoing, loving, painful, growth-inducing human interactions that take place on campus at all hours of the day and night, throughout the academic year."[1] The quality of this important process at huge public universities cannot compare with that afforded by many smaller colleges.

Further, at many large colleges (and this is equally true of many large private universities), students often have little voice in choosing their instructors. Since there may be 100 or more sections of a required course in English or history, for example, you must simply get in line and take whatever teacher you're given. Obviously, this is a bad educational value. For one thing, you will probably have no idea how good or bad your assigned professor is until it is too late to drop the course without penalty. Even worse, there will be many times when the teacher you end up with is a graduate student who may be teaching his first class. Many public schools simply don't care about the amount of education you receive for your money!

Still one more problem bears mention: at public schools, student advisement is often handled by people who don't know or don't care about what they're doing. On some

campuses, student advisement is turned over to graduate
students in the college of education, which is a serious
mistake. These students usually don't have much of an
education in the arts and sciences, so any advice they offer is
tainted by their own lack of experience and knowledge. Even
when student advisement is handled by faculty members,
however, it can be a mess. Remember our discussion about
advisors who continually pushed students into courses
related to their major during their first two years in college?
Many students have found themselves wasting two years of
their college career thanks to this advice, and many more
students have suffered in other ways at the hands of advisors
unconcerned about providing good direction.

Nothing we've said in this section is meant to suggest
that one cannot be happy or get a good education at a large
public university. Nor is it the case that the problems we've
mentioned are this bad at every state university.[2] But these
negatives ought to be considered by the families reading this
book. Get the most for your money!

Secular Private Colleges

A private college, of course, is one that is not supported by
taxpayers' money. Private colleges and universities are either
religious schools (those that have a publicly-acknowledged
religious mission or some tie to a Christian denomination) or
secular. Let's talk about secular private colleges first.

To say that a private college is secular means that it is
independent of any church, ecclesiastical, or denominational
control. Some colleges, like Princeton University and the

University of Chicago, were founded by Christian denominations, but they have since severed these ties and are rightly understood as secular schools.

Private secular schools vary greatly in size. Smaller schools of this type may have only several hundred students, while the biggest of them rival public universities in size. To mention just one example, Syracuse University has well over 20,000 students.

These schools also differ greatly in the quality of their academic programs. When many people in the U.S. are asked to identify the best colleges and universities in the country, the schools most often mentioned are private universities like Harvard, Yale, Stanford, Duke, and Vanderbilt. Notice, however, that public perception doesn't always mesh with reality. Many of the private schools that inspire a sense of awe in average citizens are actually terrible values for undergraduates. Just because a school has a good reputation does not guarantee that anyone would actually benefit from enrolling there.

Many private secular colleges are strictly four-year institutions, but some others include graduate schools that offer some of the most highly respected doctor's degrees in the country. In fact, the reputation that many of these schools have is perhaps the major reason why families that can afford it make them their college of choice. Wise families, however, rely on more than reputation when choosing a college.

Private is not synonymous with excellent; carefully examine the quality of education provided by any private secular schools on your list. Also remember that you can encounter significant hostility to evangelical Christianity on these campuses. This can also be a problem in state universities, and it can be a bigger problem in theologically liberal denominational colleges—but it is something that wise and prepared families will anticipate.

Most importantly, apply the "value criterion" to the secular private schools you consider. Do they cram hundreds of students into one course? Do they let graduate students teach many freshmen-level courses? Do they offer trained, committed advisors?

Just because a school is an expensive private college is no reason to assume that the quality of education there is better than what might be found elsewhere. Unless there is a real commitment to quality at the university, your money will not be well spent.

Hopefully, you already have discovered some private colleges—both evangelical and nonevangelical—that offer quality service. If you're having trouble finding such a school, let us take a moment to encourage you. Quality education isn't some sort of Loch Ness Monster, oft-rumored but never found. You can get good educational value at some secular private colleges, such as Hillsdale College in Hillsdale, Michigan. Although technically a secular school, Hillsdale offers an excellent Christian studies track, and serves as a ray of light in an often murky collection of private secular schools.

Nonevangelical Denominational Colleges

Private religious colleges that claim to be Protestant can be divided into those that are evangelical and those that are not.

Most Protestant colleges were evangelical at one time. As many of these schools became liberal in their understanding of the Bible and Christian beliefs, the wheat and the tares (Matthew 13:24-30) on their campuses began to grow side by side. Even after the tares took over on some of these campuses, the administration of the colleges continued to claim an evangelical commitment that no longer existed, in order to receive continued financial support from uninformed members of the denomination.

The word *evangelical*, you'll recall, only applies to Protestants who are theologically orthodox in the sense that they accept the teachings of the early Christian creeds. Evangelicals believe in the Trinity, the deity of Christ, the Incarnation, the substitutionary Atonement, the bodily resurrection of Christ, justification by faith, and other essential elements of historic Christianity. Evangelicals take the Bible to be their ultimate authority in matters of faith and practice. Evangelicals have had a religious experience usually described as a *conversion* or as being *born again*, and evangelicals are interested in leading others to the same kind of conversion experience.

There is nothing new about this list of convictions. In fact, until after the Civil War, every mainline church in America—Methodist, Presbyterian, Baptist, Lutheran, and Episcopalian—was evangelical in its theology. Slowly, the evangelical consensus in America's mainline denominations crumbled under the assault of liberal views that gradually took root in the seminaries. The attacks were directed first toward the integrity and authority of Scripture. After that important ground had been captured, the growing liberal presence in the mainline denominations began to question such essential Christian beliefs as the deity of Christ and the bodily resurrection.

Protestant liberalism is a religion without a personal God, without a divine Savior, without an inspired Bible, and without a life-transforming conversion. It is, in fact, a totally different religion that insists on retaining the Christian label. By the end of the 1920s, this new religion had gained control of denominational schools, publications, mission boards, and, eventually, total control of the mainline denominations.

The schools we label "nonevangelical denominational colleges" are the ones that are officially related in some way to the predominantly liberal mainline denominations. For example, the United Methodist Church has eighty-one colleges and eight universities. The Presbyterian Church (U.S.A.), a recent merger of the northern and southern branches of Presbyterianism, claims some seventy-one related colleges. The Evangelical Lutheran Church, a recent merger of the American Lutheran Church and the Lutheran Church in America, claims a relationship to forty-four colleges and seminaries. The Christian Church (Disciples) maintains a tie to thirty-six colleges, seminaries, and undergraduate schools of religion. There are twenty-seven colleges and universities in fellowship with the American Baptist Church. The United Church of Christ can identify more than fifty colleges with which it has some kind of relationship. There are ten Episcopalian colleges and universities.

With only a few exceptions, these denominational colleges regard themselves as enemies of evangelical

Christianity. They adhere to Protestant liberalism, or worse. In the current climate of America, this puts many of them on the side of Marxism, anti-Americanism, homosexuality, abortion, and radical feminism.

In fact, if it were not for the fact that these schools still retain some kind of tie to a Christian denomination, it would be difficult to find any justification for regarding them as Christian colleges. Many faculty members at these schools believe undermining evangelical Christianity is their most important task. As James Davison Hunter points out, "Christian higher education historically evolved into precisely the opposite of what it was supposed to be, that is, into bastions of secularity if not anti-Christian sentiment."[3]

Many of these liberal, church-related colleges played an important role in the movement of their denominations away from the historic Christian faith. Colleges that had been established to defend the faith became the tool by which that faith was undermined and largely removed from the mainline churches. Many of the people associated with these schools continue to see themselves in this role. Pity the innocent, uninformed, and unprepared evangelical student who wanders into the path of these people. Educating such a young person, for these professors, is synonymous with getting him to reject his evangelical faith.

It is for this reason that we find it difficult to recommend one of these theologically liberal schools. Many of them are far more hostile to biblical Christianity than secular colleges. And because students often enter such "Christian" colleges with their guard down, it is much easier for such schools to negatively affect the religious beliefs of that student. At least evangelicals who attend secular colleges know they will have to defend their faith!

Conclusion

Most evangelical young people choose to enroll at one of the types of schools discussed in this chapter. Their evaluations of their colleges—along with the effect those schools may have had on their Christian beliefs—are as varied as the colleges they attended. None of us should be surprised to hear that the same college has had a vastly different effect on different students. Some evangelical students can walk through firestorms of anti-Christian sentiment and emerge not only with their faith intact, but actually stronger. Other evangelicals are crippled by very trivial attacks on their faith.

Perhaps you feel that you can survive, and even thrive, at a non-Christian college. Perhaps you will. But consider: is the best education steeped in worldviews based on error, or is the best education grounded firmly on the foundation of all knowledge and wisdom (Jesus Christ)? Can education without Christ at its center be coherent or consistent?

These are not small matters. It bears repeating: your college choice should be bathed in prayer. Perhaps God intends to use you in a "missionary" capacity on a secular campus—that's fine! Just be certain that it is God guiding you in that direction, and not the fact that the school's football team is ranked in the top ten.

NINE

EVANGELICAL COLLEGES

Once upon a time, there was a little school in upstate New York named King's College. This conservative liberal arts college was founded by a fundamentalist named Percy Crawford. Through most of its history, King's College was regarded as a college that Bible-believing parents could trust to educate their children competently and to ground them in the Christian worldview.

But time passed and things changed. King's College hired a number of faculty members who were out of step with the college's historic stance on several important issues. Rumors spread that some of these professors wanted the college to provide abortion counseling for female students and condom machines for male students. Rumors also persisted that some faculty held views about ethics that were inconsistent with biblical teaching.

A new president worked to remove the dissenting teachers, but it was too late. Because of a number of problems, many of them related to faculty troubles, King's College was forced to close in December, 1994. The story's ending is sad, except for several of the terminated professors: some were quickly hired by other "evangelical" colleges.

This story is no fairy tale. It really happened, and it serves as a warning to evangelicals everywhere. There are at least two lessons to be learned.

First, we must recognize that strong evangelical colleges can be undermined quite quickly if the administration is not careful about the faculty it hires. A Christian college that was regarded as trustworthy just five years ago may have abandoned vital elements of its Christian foundation today.

Second, notice that other "evangelical" colleges were happy to hire some of the faculty members that King's College had to let go. We live at a time when laying claim to the Christian or evangelical label is not enough; it is important that students exert some effort to see if the labels accurately describe the college.

Evangelical colleges worthy of the name make no apology for their commitment to Jesus Christ, to the inspired and authoritative Word of God, and to the essential doctrinal beliefs that have defined historic Christianity. This commitment should be evident in the doctrinal statement displayed in their catalogs, and it should be evident in the decisions and actions of the college's faculty and administration. Recently, Ron visited a Southern Baptist College and met a faculty member who admitted that the administration of his college preferred to hire non-Christian professors. Such a school has no business passing itself off as a "Christian" college!

A truly evangelical college takes pains to make sure that all of its faculty members accept its doctrinal statement. Further, the evangelical college sees no inconsistency between its Christian mission and its role as an academic institution. In accordance with 2 Corinthians 10:5, truly Christian colleges seek to help their students take captive every thought for Christ—that is, to think *well*.

This chapter will discuss the strengths and weaknesses of evangelical colleges. Though we would like to focus only on those colleges that are truly committed to the biblical worldview, the constant danger represented by "Christian" colleges that are wavering on important issues forces us to raise some red flags.

Some Strengths

There is, of course, no such thing as the perfect college; not even evangelical schools are perfect. Some schools could have stronger faculty or a better library. Some schools are excellent except for one or two departments that have abandoned essential elements of the Christian worldview. Some schools are drifting theologically, advocating this or that form of trendy liberalism.

Truly committed Christian colleges, however, come closest to providing you with the best return on your educational investment. In the first place, sound evangelical schools often demonstrate a greater commitment to academic excellence than many secular schools with better reputations (remember, reputation doesn't guarantee value). When a school takes the Bible seriously, it must honor calls to excellence found in verses like Colossians 3:23: "Whatever you do, work at it with all your heart, as working for the Lord, not for men . . ." Commitment to Christ requires commitment to excellence.

On other kinds of campuses, learning and Christianity are divorced from each other. If the Christian student wants to integrate his personal faith with what he's learning in the classroom, he has to do it himself. But solid evangelical colleges make the integration of faith and learning an essential part of their mission. When Christian professors on Christian campuses are doing their job properly, the student will be helped to see how history, literature, the natural sciences, the social sciences, and other important areas of study relate to the Christian worldview.

A truly evangelical college also can offer a better educational environment than nonevangelical colleges. One of the most important and frequently overlooked aspects of a college education is the role that being part of a small, caring community for four years plays in the development of the student. Even evangelical colleges that are missing the mark with regard to some facets of the Christian worldview can attract committed Christian students (in fact, many evangelical colleges boast student populations that are more evangelical than their faculty). Don't underestimate the importance of a college's student body! You'll spend more time with your peers than you will in class or with administrators. Attending an evangelical college assures you that you will be able to work and play with many students who are growing in Christ. In other words, evangelical schools offer communities more conducive to fellowship and "iron sharpening iron" (Proverbs 27:17).

Finally, good evangelical colleges offer an approach to education that helps the student become a whole person, enabling you to tie all the important aspects of your intellectual, moral, spiritual, and religious life together. A good college should be concerned with much more than what its students learn; it should also be concerned with the kind of men and women these students become. The ancient Greeks recognized that excellence (virtue) is not intellectual alone. The good human being is the well-rounded individual: sound of mind, strong in body, and healthy in spirit. A good college should be concerned with educating the whole human being, and this includes saying something about spiritual values.

Some Weaknesses

The right student studying at the right evangelical college can benefit in ways that no public or private, secular or liberal denominational college can begin to address. Unfortunately, we must now admit that evangelical colleges also have problems, some of them serious.

Some evangelical schools are long on spirituality but short on academics. The people running the show at some of the weaker evangelical colleges have yet to see that Christianity has nothing to fear from any area of human knowledge. Some of these colleges appear to have little interest in upgrading their faculty. We have already stated that some of the stronger colleges in the nation are evangelical colleges; we must now admit that some of the weakest schools are evangelical. When considering these schools, it is important that you look carefully at their academic commitment.

More importantly, consider an evangelical college's commitment to Christ. Too many "evangelical" schools evince a noticeable wobbling on important theological issues. Many want the public to think they're theologically sound when, in fact, they are rapidly moving away from the evangelical camp.

Many Christian parents see evangelical colleges as safe places for their children to be educated. This perception is often untrue. We know many bitter and disillusioned parents who sent their children to this or that evangelical college, believing that it was as sound as when they attended twenty years ago. To their grief, these parents learned how quickly a college can change; many saw their children abandon their faith as a result of their college experience. Occasionally these students were turned into left-wing radicals by professors who couldn't tell the difference between the message of an Old Testament prophet like Amos and the message of a social radical like Karl Marx.

This tendency of evangelical schools to jettison their Christian foundation is effectively exposed by Richard Quebedeaux in *The Worldly Evangelicals*. He begins by drawing attention to the influence of liberalism in schools associated with the Southern Baptist Convention. This claim is supported by evangelical theologian Carl F.H. Henry, who says that many Southern Baptist colleges are "no longer unapologetically Christian" and "even hire faculty members who make no profession of faith whatever."[1]

Quebedeaux also points to Oral Roberts University as an example of theological wavering in such schools. Christian colleges that elevate religious feelings and experiences above sound doctrine risk drifting away from essential Christian beliefs. In the case of ORU, several Nazarene schools and several like-minded colleges, the result is often a neo-orthodox view of God's Word. Such a view refuses to equate the words of the Bible with the Word of God, preferring instead to teach that the Bible only witnesses to or contains the Word of God. This serious error also has influenced a number of Southern Baptist colleges.

According to Quebedeaux, the governing boards of several "evangelical" colleges are aware of liberal tendencies at the schools. "They know," he writes, "that many of their faculty sign the required statement of faith tongue in cheek. The same attitude pertains to faculty and students who break the conduct code (or pledge) imposed by some colleges banning gambling, alcohol, tobacco, pot and social dancing on and off campus."[2] Quebedeaux continues:

> What does concern the governing boards of these colleges, however, is that the infringement of doctrinal standards and rules of conduct remain a local, "in house" matter. As long as professors do not publish their liberal views in widely circulated popular magazines read by conservative financial backers of these institutions, much can be tolerated.[3]

Quebedeaux shocked a lot of people by including some of the best known and most highly respected evangelical colleges in his discussion. For example, he wrote that some of the faculty at Wheaton College are "moving farther to the left, both in [their] utilization of critical methods and in the cultural attitudes and politics of its faculty."⁴ Similar opinions exist with regard to other highly regarded schools such as Calvin College, Eastern College, Westmont College, Messiah College, Anderson University, and others.

Perhaps an example will best illustrate the strange new world that can often be found on Christian college campuses. Recently Kate,⁵ a freshman at a large Christian college in the Midwest, discovered that her roommate was a lesbian. Kate sought out a member of the administration and asked for a different room. In a display typical of the political correctness that now dominates some evangelical campuses, the administrator suggested that Kate ought to feel guilty for her homophobic and intolerant attitudes. Finally, however, the administration relented and allowed Kate to move to a different dorm room.

You can find advertisements for this college in almost every major Christian magazine. What's more, you can find many other Christian colleges that have the same non-biblical attitudes regarding a whole range of issues. What would happen to the enrollment at these schools if their occasional deviances from biblical morality were widely known?

Of course, many of the faculty and administrators at such schools might object to our comments. Some might assert that a good college wants its students to draw their own conclusions about the material they have been taught. We certainly agree. But this is not what we're talking about. What we have in mind are cases where a significant change in the student's beliefs and values was precisely what some people at the college sought to produce.

What is at issue here is not education, but indoctrination. According to one writer, "Indoctrination is the order of business [at many American colleges]. One historian at the University of Massachusetts begins his classes by saying: 'This course will be consistently anti-American.'"[6]

Others may complain about what they regard as our "narrow" view of education. We disagree. We happen to believe that a good education requires the presentation of competing points of view. Students should be exposed to literature that expresses these different perspectives in the words of reputable representatives of those positions. A good education is one in which students will be exposed to beliefs and values that differ from their own. A good education may include times when students are encouraged even to question their own beliefs, since this process is often a necessary step in discovering how strong that position is. But a good education is never value-neutral; indeed, value-neutral education is a myth. Every professor bases his conclusions on certain unproven assumptions (such as faith in evolution), and the best education contrasts various belief systems with the most reasonable worldview, Christianity.

The evangelical college should have much to offer. But there will always be forces at work on these campuses that will, intentionally or not, support actions and policies that subvert their purposes. As a general rule, the best college you could attend is a Christian college dedicated to Christ and the biblical worldview—and the worst is a "Christian" college that has forgotten Christ and turned its back on the biblical worldview.

What About Schools with Strengths and Weaknesses?

Until now, we have generalized and talked largely in terms of schools at opposite ends of a continuum: the very good and the very bad. This obviously is not the entire story. Many evangelical colleges are a mixed bag, with both good and bad qualities.

Such in-between schools are more or less committed to the biblical worldview, with a few faculty members or administrators that are more interested in trendy liberal views than with God's Word. The presence of these lukewarm Christian educators does not mean that you must automatically strike the school from your working list.

For example, Ron knows a couple of evangelical schools that have one or two faculty members who teach a view known as deconstructionism. In his judgment, this view is indefensible academically and extremely dangerous theologically. Ron still recommends one of these colleges, even though he warns families to be careful of the deconstructionist professor. The second college, however, has more serious problems: it has knowingly embraced deconstructionism in its English department, it has been criticized in a national publication for its commitment to politically correct thinking,[7] and some of its professors also embrace Liberation Theology.

In the first case, the relatively isolated nature of a problematic view among an otherwise sound faculty is not reason to drop the college from one's list. In the second case, the accumulation of errors along with an administration that either supports the errors or doesn't care is reason for you to look elsewhere.

The fact that an evangelical college has a biology department that teaches evolution may not bother some Christians. Even Christians who are bothered by professors committed to evolution, however, may still choose to attend that college if they do not plan to major in biology. The strengths of a college can more than make up for its weaknesses, especially if you can dodge the weakest professors and departments.

In the following chapters, we will try to help you become a better judge of the policies and presuppositions of the professors who teach at the colleges you are still considering. For now, understand that you do not have to strike an evangelical college from your list because of one or two professors you think are misguided.

Conclusion

At this point, you may wonder why we don't identify every problem at every Christian college. The answer is simple: critiques of this kind (besides being intolerably long) would also become outdated quite quickly. Ten years ago, many of the seminaries in Ron's denomination (the Southern Baptist Convention) were sympathetic to a variety of liberal ideas.

Thanks to a dramatic change in leadership at the top of the denomination, the present administrations at some of these schools have begun a major turn-around. These schools still have a long way to go, but older critiques of these schools must be revised or put on hold for a while.[8]

You may also wonder why we don't produce a long list of evangelical colleges that are theologically and academically sound. For one thing, such a list would *not* be very long. When parents and students ask advice about this or that college, we often have to begin with warnings about problems at the school. We have decided to mention three colleges we often recommend, two of them evangelical and one of them secular. Please realize that these are hardly the only colleges worthy of your consideration, and that none of these schools might be the right place for you.

The secular school, Hillsdale College, was described in the previous chapter. One of the Christian schools we both like is Bryan College in Dayton, Tennessee. We appreciate Bryan's commitment to integrate learning at every level with the biblical worldview. The president of Bryan College, William Brown, co-authored an important book on worldview thinking. The second Christian school we often recommend is Liberty University in Lynchburg, Virginia. Liberty recently withstood some serious financial trials, but seems to have weathered the storm. It has a fine faculty, an adequate physical plant and a large student body, for those who think size is important.

The rest of this book will equip you to critique the presuppositions and worldviews that you'll find at the schools left on your working list. Because you will encounter these various belief systems wherever you go, it's best to begin to understand them now. Even if you have selected a college that you are convinced is committed to Christianity, understanding these other worldviews will make you a better student. If you still have not selected the school you will attend, understanding the concepts in the following chapters will help you evaluate the schools left on your list.

TEN

WEARING THE RIGHT GLASSES

By now, you should be very close to selecting the best college for you. Remember, however, that choosing the college is only part of the battle. The real challenge begins when you step on campus: Will you stand firm for Christ? In order to stand firm in an environment so fraught with pitfalls, you must understand certain things about yourself and the people around you.

As you find your way around campus, pay close attention to your fellow students and professors. Did you notice? They, like you, are wearing invisible glasses. Every person you see, from the college president on down, is wearing them.

These invisible glasses serve an important purpose: they help the person wearing them to "see" the world. Some people see the world clearly, because they are wearing the right pair of glasses, and others see the world in a distorted way, because their glasses are all wrong. Occasionally, people will trade in one pair of glasses for another, because they think the new pair will help them see better. Sometimes they are right, and sometimes they are wrong.

These invisible glasses, of course, are our worldviews—our ways of interpreting all of reality.[1] If we believe that Buddha was the Enlightened One who can teach us how to live and how to think, we own one set of glasses. If we believe that Jesus Christ is the Way, the Truth, and the Life, we own a different set of glasses. People may attempt to mix two or more worldviews together to create a new worldview, but this is just as silly as wearing two pairs of glasses to adjust your vision—if one pair doesn't give you a clear version of reality, then the second pair will only distort it more.

Everyone has a worldview. What's more, every worldview is religious, in the sense that they reflect ultimate commitments of the heart. In *Worldviews in Conflict*, Ron argues that the Christian worldview is intellectually superior to any competing system. Some students trade in their Christian worldview when they reach college because they believe they have "outgrown" faith and need only rely on reason. This is terrible reasoning! Every worldview requires faith; the wise student simply chooses the worldview that reflects the most reasonable faith.

Throughout this book, we have encouraged you to avoid being taken captive by deceitful worldviews. We say this not because we expect you to make a poor college choice, but because these deceitful worldviews are on every campus—even at the best Christian college in the nation— and every year students who thought they were Christians trade in their good glasses for faulty pairs that twist reality. Sometimes professors bully students into changing their worldview; sometimes fellow students make another worldview appear exciting or sophisticated. Whatever the reason, trading the truth of Christianity for any lie is unwise and dangerous.

To survive (and thrive) on campus, you should be aware of some of the snares along the way. If you understand the basics of the other worldviews vying for your allegiance, then you will better understand why Christianity is a much more reasonable way of looking at the world. The rest of this chapter will focus on some of the most popular false worldviews, so that you will be able to recognize them when you encounter them.

Secular Humanism

People who adhere to the Secular Humanist worldview deny the existence of God and anything else supernatural (this philosophical position is called *naturalism*). The basic claim of naturalism is that "Nothing exists outside the material, mechanical, natural order."

For naturalists, the universe is a closed box. Everything that happens inside the box is explainable in terms of other things that exist within the box. Nothing exists outside the box; therefore, nothing outside the universe can cause anything that happens inside the universe.

Given such a philosophy, it is small wonder that Secular Humanists object to major elements of the Christian worldview. Any naturalist is precluded from believing in

God, souls, angels, miracles, prayer, providence, immortal-
ity, heaven, sin, conscience, free will and salvation, as
Christians normally understand these notions. Such things
cannot exist for the Humanist because they cannot be seen—
they have no material form. For the Secular Humanist,
seeing is literally believing. If it can't be tested, studied, and
measured, it doesn't exist.

Most Secular Humanists never try to prove that
naturalism is true—for good reason. Such a proof is
impossible, because it must rely on the laws of logic—
immaterial laws that, according to the naturalist, should not
exist! The Humanist's rejection of God and everything else
supernatural is a reflection of his religious commitment to a
naturalistic philosophy.

The best definition of Secular Humanism is provided
by the first *Humanist Manifesto*:

> Humanists regard the universe as self-
> existing and not created. . . . Humanism
> asserts that the nature of the universe
> depicted by modern science makes unaccept-
> able any supernatural cosmic guarantees of
> human value. . . . Religious humanism
> considers the complete realization of human
> personality to be the end of man's life and
> seeks its development and fulfillment in the
> here and now. . . . In place of the old attitudes
> involved in worship and prayer the humanist
> finds his religious emotions expressed in a
> heightened sense of personal life and in a

cooperative effort to promote social well-being.... Man is at last becoming aware that he alone is responsible for the realization of the world of his dreams, that he has within himself the power for its achievement.[2]

In this view, humankind usurps the place of God. Humanism is, in the words of an ancient Greek philosopher, the belief that man (not God) is the measure of all things. With man as the measure, ethics becomes relative, the government becomes sovereign, and it is a short road to totalitarianism.

Marxism

You may not know very many people who refer to themselves as Secular Humanists. More often, folks describe themselves as atheists or agnostics (which is usually synonymous with Secular Humanism) or as some special kind of atheist, like a Marxist.

One of the biggest problems with Marxism is that it means so many different things to so many people. Because Karl Marx formulated his worldview inconsistently, and because he often contradicted himself, people tend to "interpret" Marx in different ways.

Some of the interpretations of Marx are fairly comprehensive, and thus form a complete worldview. The system that enslaved the former Soviet Union and many Eastern bloc countries (and still enslaves Cuba), Marxism/Leninism, is an example of a Marxist worldview.[3] Other interpretations are less complete, and are often used simply as tools to attack objective truth. The four most common interpretations of Marx will be discussed in the following chapter.

For now, it is enough to understand that any variation of Marxism is based on the perception that some kind of oppression dominates our world, and that the most important thing man can do is eradicate this oppression. Traditionally, Marxists assert that all property-owners oppress the workers. Other interpretations of Marx describe the oppression of males over females, or whites over non-whites.

Eastern Mysticism

Both Marxism and Secular Humanism are based on an atheistic theology. Other worldviews gaining popularity in the United States are based on pantheism—the belief that everything is God. Many college students and professors embrace pantheistic Eastern religions like Buddhism. One feature of this mysticism is the claim that God (or Ultimate Reality) lies beyond the limits of human knowledge, and therefore we must seek the ultimate in the inner depths of our own being. For some, this search is supposedly aided by the use of drugs. Others rely on meditation, fire-walking, or hypnosis.

There are too many versions of this way of thinking to discuss in detail. Suffice it to say that they share many of the same characteristics: a glorification of selfishness, moral relativism, faith in evolution, and a rejection of logic. This last facet is perhaps the most frustrating for the Christian, because it allows adherents to cling to logical inconsistencies even when confronted with them. One cannot reason a mystic toward the truth because the highest "truth," they feel, is beyond human reason. Ironically, these same people reject Christianity because, they say, it is so "unreasonable."

The New Age Movement

Couple Eastern mysticism with modern American wishful thinking, and you arrive at the hottest worldview in our culture: the New Age. As many scholars have noted, there is really nothing "new" about the New Age—it borrows virtually all of its foundation from Buddhism or Hinduism, and then provides the instant gratification of assuring us that we are all on the fast track to godhood.

The best summation of this worldview was provided by one of its leading proponents, Shirley MacLaine. In her TV miniseries "Out on a Limb," MacLaine describes her own spiritual journey, which climaxes on a beach. At this point, her guru encourages her to chant the assertion that she is God. When MacLaine tells her guru that she can't say that, he responds, "See how little you think of yourself?" Spurred on by this encouragement, MacLaine triumphantly faces the ocean and begins to yell, "I am God!" Apparently, her self-esteem has been repaired.

According to the New Age religion, everything is God (including every person), so the sooner we get in touch with our godhood the better. When enough people achieve this higher consciousness, the world will experience a spiritual leap into a "new age" of peace and unity.

Eventually, we will all be merged into the God-consciousness where all is one, including good and bad, love and hate, fear and courage. Such a unity is our evolutionary goal.

Because of its ties to Eastern mysticism, the New Age movement borrows all of the traditional Eastern methods of self-discovery, including fire-walking, and also embraces reincarnation, spiritism, and many beliefs and practices of pagan religions. Really, any religion except Christianity can work for the New Ager, as long as it helps you discover your godhood. The advice provided by New Age icon Joseph Campbell, "follow your bliss," is the only absolute for proponents of this worldview.

Many people accept this philosophy without actually understanding what they have bought into. The notion that "there are many paths to God," or that we all worship the same God in our own different ways, is just a variation of the New Age worldview. This pluralistic attitude is a subtle but decisive rejection of Christianity, because the Christian worldview explicitly teaches that only those who put their trust in Jesus Christ can be saved (John 14:6).

Tragically, the pluralistic view thrives at some "Christian" colleges, including many affiliated with mainline denominations. The irony is overwhelming: Christianity, the one worldview that is radically different, is lumped together with all other worldviews as an equally valid means of reaching heaven. While New Agers recognize this distinction and rebel against biblical Christianity, some "Christian" colleges treat other religions as trustworthy methods for discovering God.

One final warning about the New Age: even though

its proponents reject traditional Christianity, they still use Christian language and symbols when describing their beliefs. For example, New Agers talk about a "God," and sometimes even "salvation," and many of them seem to revere Jesus Christ and the Bible. This makes the New Age seem, on the surface, to be quite similar to Christianity, when in fact it is diametrically opposed. When New Age advocates talk reverently about Jesus, they do so only because they regard Him as another prophet of New Age consciousness. When they call the Bible a sacred text, they are lumping it together with all the other works they consider "sacred": the Koran, the writings of Confucius, etc.

The Bible declares itself to be the complete Word of God, and Christ proclaimed that He is the only Way! Those who claim to revere the God of the Bible while denying His most basic assertions are simply deceiving themselves.

Cults

The New Age worldview is not the only worldview, however, that pretends to worship the God of the Bible. Many cults that call themselves Christian also use Christian language and claim to revere the one true God—but their words mean something entirely different. The most obvious cults include The Church of Jesus Christ of Latter-day Saints (Mormons), Jehovah's Witnesses, the Unification Church (Moonies), and Christian Science.

Most members of these cults adamantly declare themselves to be Christians, but they have rejected every important element of Christian doctrine. For example, "The

Church of Jesus Christ of Latter-day Saints discounts the notion of Original Sin and its ascribed negative impact on humanity," according to Mormon Apostle M. Russell Ballard. He continues, "Indeed, we honor and respect Adam and Eve for their wisdom and foresight."[4] Such a view is antithetical to the Christian position that one man brought death into the world, and one Man brought life (Romans 5:18-19).

Cults generally twist Christianity in four important ways, as outlined by Summit Ministries Researcher Kevin Bywater:

• They add to the Word of God. (2 Timothy 3:16-17)
• They subtract from the deity of Jesus Christ, and deny the doctrine of the Trinity. (John 1:1)
• They multiply the terms of salvation. (Ephesians 2:6-10)
• They divide their followers' loyalties between God and the organization. (1 Corinthians 7:23-24)[5]

Obviously, committing even one of these errors destroys the gospel message. Cults that propagate these lies preach exactly the opposite of the good news of the Bible—requiring men and women to work to save themselves, rather than relying on God's grace. If we must work to save ourselves, Christ's ultimate sacrifice becomes meaningless, and Christianity loses all its power.

Theological Liberalism

There is, of course, another way to twist the Christian message: create what C.S. Lewis called the "milk and water"

version. Make everyone feel good by removing all the
challenging, difficult teachings of the Bible. This approach,
which generally can be called theological liberalism, takes
many forms. Often it is indistinguishable from Secular
Humanism or the pluralism of the New Age movement.

If you take a religion course at a secular or pseudo-
Christian college, you will certainly encounter liberal
theologians. For most of the nineteenth and twentieth
centuries, theological liberals worked to undermine the
foundation of America's large Protestant denominations,
denying every central belief of the Christian faith.[6] They
rejected the belief in the Trinity, the deity of Jesus Christ, the
Incarnation, the Atonement, and the bodily resurrection of
Jesus. They denied that the Bible is the inspired and infallible
Word of God.

Theological liberalism is still pervasive today, but
modern proponents have learned to use language that
disguises the true nature of their unbelief. Today they might
occasionally talk about the resurrection of Jesus—but they
don't mean His physical resurrection! Instead, they mean
something warm and fuzzy and non-threatening: after His
death, Jesus continued to live on in the memory of his
followers. Such a belief has nothing to do with the kind of
resurrection we find described in the New Testament.[7]

Generally, theological liberalism takes on one of
three forms: Neo-orthodoxy, Process Theology, or
Liberation Theology. We will discuss each version briefly, so
that you will be able to recognize it when you see it.
However, you should also realize that these positions often
borrow important concepts from each other. Today, it's

tragically easy to find people who defend a synthesis of Process Theology, Liberation Theology, and radical feminism with a decidedly sub-Christian view of the Bible.

For much of the first half of the twentieth-century, old-fashioned theological liberals were content to deny that the Bible was the Word of God. In their view, the Bible was a human document that was full of errors. In the last fifty years, however, a more subtle attack has replaced this blatant liberalism. This new worldview is called *Neo-orthodoxy*, because it claims to represent a position somewhere between the unbelief of the old liberalism and the orthodoxy of evangelicals.

The central idea behind the Neo-orthodox view is the refusal to recognize the Bible as the revealed Word of God. Neo-orthodox professors want students to believe that the Bible *becomes* the Word of God under certain circumstances. We must never, they insist, confuse the Bible with the Word of God. The Word of God is what God says to us "in our hearts" when we read the Bible or have religious experiences. Thus, the Word of God is a totally subjective experience. For the Neo-orthodox, the Bible is only an instrument—perhaps one of many—through which the Word of God might come to us. Some liberal Protestants go so far as to claim that the Word of God might come to us through music and art, rather than the Bible.

James Davison Hunter explains the central problem with this worldview:

> [N]eo-orthodoxy has devalued the historicity
> of the biblical account of historical events.

The crucial issue from this standpoint is not that those events actually occurred but simply that God is trying to teach us something of spiritual significance by the symbolism of these stories. Thus, for example, the believer does not have to be concerned whether or not the origin of the world occurred precisely in the manner described in the Book of Genesis. What is central is that the believer learns from this that, among other things, God is the source and creator of life. In its logical extreme, this form of theologizing would conclude that it is unimportant whether the Resurrection of Christ actually occurred, but merely that God is teaching the believer something of tremendous importance by this story.[8]

Because the Neo-orthodox view of the Bible is taught at so many colleges that claim to be Christian, it is wise to be prepared on this issue. Neo-orthodoxy is a popular fad at most Southern Baptist and Nazarene colleges. Be on the watch for professors who deny that the Bible *is* the Word of God but only *becomes* the Word of God under certain conditions.

The second form of theological liberalism, *Process Theology*, is a difficult system to understand. As its name suggests, Process Theology begins with the assumption that all of reality (including God) is characterized by change. Many Process thinkers argue that there are serious problems with a view of God that emphasizes God's immutability or unchangeableness. A God who is incapable of change, they say, cannot be the loving and caring God of the Bible.

There are two important ways to identify a Process Theologian. Some advocates of this worldview deny the Christian teaching that God created the world from nothing. These theologians teach that both God and the world are eternal, and are just different aspects of the same Reality. God can be thought of, they say, as the soul of the world— and the world as the body of God. The world and God need each other.

You can also recognize a Process Theologian by his views about God and the future. These liberal theologians claim that God cannot know the future actions of human beings. God must adapt to the changes brought about by human beings on earth. This tenet of Process Theology has been taught on many "evangelical" campuses, including Southern Baptist schools, Anderson University, and Azusa Pacific University.

The problems with this theory are manifold. If God cannot know the future, then He cannot control the future. Moreover, He cannot answer prayer, nor can He know ahead of time which human beings will exist or will believe in Him. God, for the Process Theologian, is little more than a stop-gap: never in control, but always rushing around and fixing things as best He can. The all-powerful, all-knowing God of the Bible is replaced by a celestial butler who tidies up after us.

The third form of theological liberalism is called *Liberation Theology*. This complex worldview downplays the historic, doctrinal side of Christianity and emphasizes instead Christian action (*praxis*) on behalf of poor and oppressed people.[9] Liberation Theology can appear very attractive to dedicated Christian students who find it easy to identify with the underdogs of the world.

This is exactly what Liberation Theologians want. While the uninformed Christian focuses on this harmless assertion that we should serve others, the Liberation Theologian smuggles in poisonous errors. Many Roman Catholic Liberation Theologians have been condemned by the Vatican for denying the atonement and the resurrection. Protestant Liberation thinkers are heretical in similar ways.

Ultimately, most Liberation Theologians mix the Christian worldview with Marxism, creating an incoherent mess that encourages such un-Christian actions as supporting violent revolutions. Liberation Theology in practice provides the exact opposite of liberation: its distortion or rejection of the gospel means that it cannot offer human beings liberation from sin; its frequent disinterest in democracy means that it cannot offer liberation from tyranny; and its obsession with socialism means that it cannot offer liberation from poverty.

Many readers would be surprised to see a list of all the evangelical colleges and seminaries where some variety of Christian Marxism is endorsed. What would not surprise you is the havoc this view wreaks on Christianity. Virtually every aspect of the Christian worldview—from politics to economics to ethics—is shattered by this illogical marriage of Christianity to a false worldview.

Conclusion

Not every professor at every college is a radical fanatic bent
on turning you into an intellectual zombie. Many professors
are honest men trying to teach their subject matter. Many
professors are committed Christians who want to help you
better understand your Christian worldview.

But regardless of which college you attend, you will
also run into professors and students whose worldviews
differ from yours. As you interact with these people, you will
have a choice: compromise, or rely on God's revealed Word
as your foundation (and perhaps in the process help them to
embrace the Christian worldview!). If you understand that
everyone has a worldview, and you have a general idea of
what the false worldviews look like, it will be a lot easier for
you to stand firm in your faith. Properly prepared Christian
students can attend college anywhere and still stand firm.

This does not mean that you have to become an
expert in everything from theology to apologetics[10] to
philosophy to worldview analysis. What it does mean is that
you should have a basic grasp of the different systems of
thought, and some understanding of where to look when
you've been challenged by proponents of false worldviews.
This book will help you with both objectives, by introducing
you to various ideas in this chapter and the next, and by
providing a bibliography for further study at the end of this
book. If you arrive at your college campus and find that you
need to know more about the New Age movement, simply
refer back to our bibliography and check out one of the books
listed there. Good thinkers don't know everything; often

they just know where to look to find the information they need.

The next chapter will prepare you for some of the modern methods used by college professors to assault the Christian worldview. These methods and ideas usually have their foundation in one or more of the false worldviews discussed in this chapter, though their connection is often disguised. While you need not know everything about the concepts described in the next chapter, attending college without some awareness of these concepts would be like crossing the Sahara Desert without sunscreen.

ELEVEN

CAMPUS RADICALS

You aren't really prepared for college until you realize how many college profs have become activists for a radical left-wing political and cultural agenda. Many of these professors teach little or nothing in terms of traditional subject matter, especially in areas like freshman English, sociology and history. Instead, they use their position and power to "radicalize" their students, breaking down their traditional beliefs and making them susceptible to false worldviews.

According to University of Massachusetts professor Paul Hollander, the single major source of left-wing culture in America is the college campus. He writes, "Even if the majority of the students in the nation today do not subscribe to [this] mentality, large and vocal portions of their teachers do, especially in the humanities and social sciences."[1] Hollander's assertions are supported by William Simon, a former secretary of the U.S. Treasury. Simon uses Stanford University as the most obvious example of the radical agenda:

Stanford's pattern of scholastic bias and
academic double standards is, by now, well-
established. In 1983, the school expelled a
scholar from the PhD program for document-
ing the Chinese policy of massive, coerced
abortions. Earlier this year [1988], it
removed several books from its core Western
civilization reading list because of the sex or
race of their authors.[2]

Simon goes on to provide numerous examples
supporting his claim that "colleges are, once again, becoming
a battleground . . . with the radicals trampling the right of free
expression and bullying those who do not share their zealotry
to place ideology over the pursuit of truth."[3]

This leftist zealotry can spring from any of the false
worldviews—from Hinduism to the New Age movement to
Secular Humanism—but it is especially connected to the
Marxist worldview.

Isn't Marxism dead? Didn't we see the Berlin Wall
fall and whole nations rejoice? Well . . . yes and no. Yes,
anyone who has lived under a Marxist regime would
celebrate the downfall of Marxism—but incredibly, many
Western intellectuals did not rejoice, because they still see
Marxism as the plan of salvation for humanity.

This irony did not escape one journalist: "When
American students return to U.S. colleges and universities [in
the fall of 1989]," Georgie Anne Geyer wrote, "they will
make an extraordinary voyage—from a summer where the
whole world was denouncing and renouncing Marxism to

just about the only place where self-righteous Marxists still exist and thrive."[4] According to an article in *U.S. News and World Report*, there are more than 10,000 Marxists teaching on American college campuses.[5] "The Marxist academics are today's power elite in the universities" says Arnold Beichman, "and [because of] the magic of the tenure system they have become self-perpetuating. . . . It has successfully substituted Marxist social change as the goal of learning, instead of a search for objective truth."[6]

Marxists (or adherents to other false worldviews) are not interested in an education that opens the American mind or heart. Their objective is to subvert truth in an effort to enlist students for their radical cause. According to Geyer, these men and women "are intellectual disgraces to a free society."[7] Unfortunately, such people control many college campuses—including some "Christian" college campuses. Many of these professors are Marxists, while many others are Secular Humanists, New Agers, or something equally bad. Regardless of their specific false worldview, most professors will employ a few radical techniques to assault objective truth. Once they have removed a students' faith in objective truth, it is very easy for them to manipulate the student in any way they please.

If you are to thrive on the college campus, you must be able to recognize the attacks on God's truth described throughout the rest of this chapter. Some of these concepts will seem difficult—most will appear downright bizarre—but you need not understand everything about them. Just be able to recognize the attacks when you see them, and know where to look for more information.

The Four Faces of Marxism

Because so much of the radical agenda springs from some interpretation of Karl Marx, it's best to begin by understanding the different "faces" of Marxism. When you find someone claiming a Marxist motivation for their actions, you cannot adequately respond to them until you discover what type of Marxism they embrace.

The first face, the only interpretation of Marx that is actually a complete worldview, is *Marxism/Leninism.* This interpretation was the official position of V.I. Lenin and the Bolsheviks, who used it to justify the October Revolution of 1917 (which marked the beginning of the Soviet Union). There is no place for democracy in this version of Marxism; instead, it is assumed that the communist party always knows what is best for the workers, whether the workers agree or not. Marxism/Leninism is totalitarian by definition, and relies on violent revolution. Castro's Cuba and all of its evils are a good example of Leninism in action.

Other radicals reject this Leninist interpretation of Marx, however, and adapt Marx's theories to suit their own political or social agendas. These other faces of Marxism generally fall into three categories: social-democratic Marxism, neo-Marxism, and what we call chameleon Marxism. None of these theories are, generally speaking, total worldviews—that is, they don't seek to answer all the questions about reality—but they are convenient frameworks for assaulting important truths.

For several decades after Marx's death, a number of people in Great Britain taught that his ideas were compatible with democracy and political freedom. These people, *social-democratic Marxists* (or Fabian Socialists), believed the "revolution" Marx and his colleague Frederick Engels described could be realized through peaceful means such as democratic elections. As Marxism/Leninism was put into practice by Lenin and Joseph Stalin in the Soviet Union (and its basic reliance on violence became more apparent), many social-democratic Marxists in Great Britain and the United States preferred to be known simply as socialists. Socialism—the belief that an economic system should be planned and controlled rather than driven by the free market—is alive and well on college campuses today, though many socialists would deny any ties to Marxism (many Secular Humanists are socialists).

Neo-Marxism is a major departure from traditional Marxism/Leninism and social-democratic Marxism. The most basic distinction between neo-Marxism and other varieties is its emphasis on the concept of alienation.[8] Neo-Marxists claim that several early (1843-1844) unpublished writings by Marx identify four different but related forms of worker alienation.

According to this theory, the wrong economic system—capitalism—begins by causing the worker to become alienated from that which he produces. Because capitalism creates false needs and provides false satisfactions, workers are manipulated into wanting things and then seduced into buying them. Next, capitalism causes the worker to become estranged from the labor process itself. Just look at how many men and women hate their jobs! Third, the worker under capitalism becomes alienated from other men and women, a fact easily observed by noting the widespread competitiveness, hostility, and animosity among human beings. Finally, the worker not only becomes alienated from what he produces, from his work, and from other workers—he even becomes alienated from himself.

All four forms of human alienation are serious business—no Christian would dispute that. The problem arises, however, when we ask ourselves how Marx fits into the picture. Why should Marx be given any credit for discovering the problem or for recommending a solution? The theory of alienation is neither unique to Marx nor original with him; it was described by a number of thinkers before him, and it was developed independently by several writers after him. Moreover, human alienation is hardly unique to capitalist societies. The assertion that capitalism is the root of all these evils can be falsified by any trip to a Marxist country—the very same alienation exists there! Human alienation is no more an exclusive effect of capitalism than is baldness or pneumonia.

Tragically, neo-Marxism is prevalent at many so-called Christian colleges. A few years ago, Ron spent several days participating in a conference with a group of sociology professors from various evangelical colleges. After just a few hours of discussion, Ron realized that everyone else in that conference room was neo-Marxist. Their professional training had so indoctrinated them that they brought Marxist assumptions with them to their teaching of sociology, little realizing the deadly problems created by those assumptions.

Tony Campolo, a well-known Christian speaker and professor of sociology at Eastern College, provides an excellent example of the neo-Marxist influence on some Christian campuses. In his book *We Have Met The Enemy, and They Are Partly Right,* Campolo spends many pages praising Marx for a number of his ideas, including those related to the claims about human alienation.[9]

Strangely missing from the discussions of alienation by Campolo and other Christian fans of Marx is any recognition of a fifth variety of human alienation, a type that Marx also conveniently ignored. Scripture teaches that every member of the human race is *alienated from God.* In fact, the Bible proclaims that all of the forms of human alienation that concern neo-Marxists result from man's more fundamental alienation from his Creator. Recognition of this Biblical truth could introduce an important new dimension into discussions of alienation. It might even lead sociology professors in Christian colleges to abandon some of their uncritical enthusiasm for Marxist and neo-Marxist concepts.

The last face of Marxism you should recognize is something we call *chameleon Marxism.* Just as the chameleon changes its color to suit its environment (thus helping it hide), so the Marxist professors of today do their best to mask their true convictions.

This new type of Marxist is bent on obliterating the past from our memory, and on rewriting history. As historian Lee Congdon explains, Marxist professors reason that if "they are to control the future, they must first take possession of the past by inducing selective amnesia and reinterpreting events in such a way as to promote contemporary political ambitions."[10]

The goal of all these chameleon Marxists is to control

human memory. Since our past helps define who and what
we are, control of what people remember results in control of
those people. If the Marxist professors are allowed to
rewrite history in Marxist terms, they will be able to guide
people toward embracing Marxism.

Why, Congdon asks, do so many college-educated
people believe that anti-communism is simplistic, just
another hangover of the Cold War? Why are many
Americans so much more critical of their own nation?
Because certain radical professors have succeeded at
indoctrinating American college students. Never mind that
in the past Marxism has created horribly repressive systems,
or that America, which is based on a Christian foundation,
has long served as the cradle of liberty. This is just part of the
past that the chameleon Marxists choose to erase.

Naturally, it is difficult to spot these chameleon
Marxists. Certain warning signs, however, should make you
suspicious. When a professor shows a real disregard for
historical facts, when he portrays all of history as a battle
between oppressed and oppressors, when he portrays
America as the primary source of evil in the world, or when
he suppresses all opinions that don't mesh with his version of
reality, it would be reasonable to assume that he is a Marxist.
At the very least, these warning signs will make you aware
that the professor is a radical with little regard for the truth.

Generally speaking, then, there are four popular
"faces" of Marxism: Marxism/Leninism, social-democratic
Marxism, neo-Marxism, and chameleon Marxism. These
theories can be coupled with a distorted Christianity to form
a schizophrenic worldview like Liberation Theology, or they

can be used simply as tools to undermine truth.

In addition to these tools, Marxists of any variety may use some of the tools described below. Chameleon Marxists are especially fond of the politically correct movement and deconstructionism. However, the following tools may also be used by Secular Humanists, New Agers, or proponents of other false worldviews.

Deconstructionism

It is practically impossible for you to make it through four years of college without encountering deconstructionism. In its simplest terms, deconstructionism is the teaching that *no one can ever know the meaning of any written text.* People who swallow this theory believe the act of interpretation is more important than the text—that is, the text has no meaning and the interpretation is the only source of meaning. Naturally, there can be no such thing as a correct interpretation—if the person who wrote the text can't infuse it with one distinct meaning, how could you?

The deconstructionist mentality is most popular in English departments, though its influence has recently spread to other liberal arts, the social sciences, and even law. The problem with deconstructionism can be discovered simply by reflecting on the italicized words in the preceding paragraph. Those words, of course, constitute a written text, something the deconstructionist tells us no one can really understand. But this supposedly meaningless combination of words is the basic thesis of deconstructionism!

If deconstructionists were really serious about their

work, they would recognize that their own theory demands that no one will ever understand what the deconstructionists say or write. Are they kidding? Challenge them, and you will find out exactly how serious they are. Any efforts to treat written texts as if they have inherent meaning will result in a lot of heartache and failing grades. (Of course, you could always try to convince your parents that they should interpret the "F" on your report card as an "A.")

Unfortunately, a student's need to pass a course often forces him to play the deconstructionist's game. Several years ago, a young lady we'll call Barb enrolled in a freshman literature class taught by a fanatical deconstructionist. Barb quickly recognized the nonsense she was being taught but had an obvious interest in passing the course, so she played along. Near the end of the course, the professor announced that the final exam would cover *Moby Dick* by Herman Melville. Barb thought it was time to show the professor the absurdity of his views, so she decided to come up with the craziest interpretation of *Moby Dick* she could. On exam day, Barb wrote, "Moby Dick is the Republic of Ireland." She then spent ninety minutes completing the exam, making up her interpretation as she went along. Did the professor recognize the absurdity? Of course not. Barb received an "A" for her "interpretation." And why not? If meaning is subjective, no interpretation has any advantage over any other.

Deconstructionists must believe that no one, not even themselves, can understand literary texts—even their *own* texts. All of the writings of deconstructionists in which they analyze other authors are only "subjective musings." But why should anyone care? And even if we did care about this or that author, the deconstructionist's own principles would prevent us from understanding those musings. Deconstructionism turns out to be a self-refuting theory.

As silly as this theory is, it is still extremely dangerous to the students who swallow it. As soon as you believe that truth is relative—a basic assumption for deconstructionists—you must accept that ethics is relative, too. No longer do absolute right and wrong exist—instead, you'll be forced to "create your own meaning" by following your own emotions. Following your emotions, however, is a dangerous occupation in a universe created by One who expects certain thoughts and actions from His creations.

Radical Feminism

Radical feminists are also adept at destroying a student's faith in objective truth. Though feminism is often understood simply as the belief that discrimination against any person on the basis of sex is wrong, radical feminism means a great deal more.   Radical feminism has as its ultimate goal the elimination of all distinctions between the sexes.

As Christina Hoff Sommers explains, radical feminists "share an ideal of a genderless culture that inspires their rejection of such entrenched social arrangements as the family, marriage and maternal responsibilities for child rearing. They also call not only for a radical re-ordering of society but . . . a revolution in knowledge itself, which would extirpate masculine bias, replacing the 'male-centered' [college curriculum] with a new curriculum inspired by a radical feminist perspective."[11]

Radical feminists believe that they possess a special way of understanding reality, a power lacking in men and even non-feminist women. This new consciousness gives them unique types of knowledge that, among other things, make it possible for them to explain for the first time in history the true relationship between men and women. The radical feminist places her experiences and her "understanding" above God's revelation in the Bible.

As you may have guessed, this exaltation of self and the "new consciousness" fits nicely with the New Age worldview. New Agers love radical feminism's call for "unity" (erasing distinctions between the sexes), and their rejection of traditional religions like Christianity because such religions are supposedly "patriarchal" or male-dominated. By rejecting traditional religion, many radical feminists open the door for the New Age practices of self-worship and worship of the goddess Mother Earth, or Gaia. Radical feminism is compatible with such pantheism, and also with paganism. Witchcraft is often popular with radical feminist leaders.

Radical feminists also reject logic (again, a nice fit with the New Age worldview!), because they perceive the laws of logic as a male-chauvinist tool to oppress women. Of course, if they reject logic they can hardly argue that students should embrace radical feminism, since reason flaunts the very precepts of radical feminism. Nor can they contend that Christianity is unreasonable. The best a radical feminist can do is reject Christianity because it doesn't "feel" right. Anyone could reject radical feminism on the same grounds.

Multiculturalism

Multiculturalism sounds innocent enough. Shouldn't everyone have an open-minded attitude towards other cultures? But the agenda of multiculturalists is far more sinister than simply encouraging students to study the best aspects of different cultures. In fact, the agenda of multiculturalists is just the opposite.

Multiculturalist professors and administrators are not interested in discovering the "beautiful" or the "true" in any culture—instead they preach that all cultures are *equally good*—thereby destroying the concept of an absolute standard. We may not judge another culture, because it is as good as any other culture. Forget your standard—God's Word—and just accept the cultures for what they are.

In the hands of multiculturalists teaching literature, for example, all of the great classics of Western literature are denied any special standing. Books written by totally unknown representatives of your professor's pet culture are treated as though they are as valuable as books by Plato, John Milton, or Alexander Solzhenitsyn. You might spend a little time reading William Shakespeare, but then you should spend an equal amount of time reading mediocre books by obscure authors from other cultures.

At least, that's the way multiculturalism is supposed to work. As it turns out, however, multiculturalism is even worse than this. In practice, multiculturalists actually treat one civilization as unequal to all other cultures—that is, as drastically inferior to the rest of the world. What civilization is so devoid of value? Western civilization, of course!

Multiculturalists have no time for dead, white males like Edmund Burke or George Washington—such men just helped perpetuate the greedy, male-dominated, shallow societies in America and England today.   Rather, multiculturalists will spend large portions of your class time exalting their pet cultures at the expense of Western civilization.

A fine example of this kind of thinking was outlined in a publication Ron received from Syracuse University. An article in this alumni magazine trumpeted recent changes to their English curriculum, while assuring the reader that the department had not abandoned the classics. "The revamped curriculum will cover the classics," the article stated, "but also will include the study of films, television shows, popular novels, and even comic strips."[12] Translation: the Syracuse English department now regards television shows and comic strips as the equal of the great classics of Western literature. And it gets worse. The article went on to say that "Works by Shakespeare, Chaucer, Homer, Joyce, and other 'old white boys,' [note the condescending sarcasm]. . . will be studied not only for their artistic merits, but also in the context of the political, cultural, and historical forces that shaped their work."[13]   In other words, left-wing multiculturalist professors will now use an occasional classic text to further demonstrate the alleged bankruptcy of Western civilization. Though the language is carefully selected to avoid enraging conservative donors, the message is clear.   Western civilization is out; the only reason America is of any interest is because it demonstrates how *not* to build a society.

As with all other campus radicals, truth is

unimportant to the multiculturalist. If it suits his views to claim that bifocals were invented in Africa rather than America, then the multiculturalist will teach it. Truth is never absolute for these radicals; it is simply something you manipulate to create your own reality.

Political Correctness

By now you are probably suspicious that college isn't what it used to be. And it gets worse: as the politically correct movement gains momentum, college becomes even more treacherous. If you are unfortunate enough to attend a college where the faculty and administration have surrendered to this ideology, you will soon find that any deviation from the thinking prescribed by your radical professors will have dire consequences. One University of Washington student who questioned a professor's statistics about lesbians, for example, received this response: "Why are you challenging me? Get away from me. Just leave me alone." The next day, the student found two campus police officers waiting for him at the classroom door; the officers informed him that he was banned from the class, and escorted him away.[14]

If you choose to play along rather than suffer such consequences, you pay a very high price: you must pretend to think exactly the way your professors want you to think. To be politically correct, you must teach yourself to approve of homosexuality, left-wing politics, left-wing economics, abortion, liberal politicians, anti-Christian religious beliefs, and radical feminism. But woe unto any student who dares to nurture positive attitudes toward the Bible, Christianity, capitalism, America, conservative politicians (especially Ronald Reagan), Rush Limbaugh, the writings of dead white European males, the pro-life movement, family values, sexual abstinence . . . you get the picture.

If you think all this sounds like much of American higher education is run by thought-police, congratulations—you understand what this chapter is all about.

Conclusion

Obviously, you don't want to attend a college with too many professors or administrators who embrace the radical attitudes described in this chapter. To avoid such a situation, you should do everything you can to ensure that the colleges left on your working list are relatively radical-free.

Finding this out is not particularly difficult, though it will require some work. If you're concerned that a particular college might sanction multiculturalism, check to see which books are studied in their literature and Western civilization courses (if Madonna's name occurs more than William Shakespeare's does,[15] you know you're in trouble). Worried about deconstructionism? Talk to professors in the English, history, and sociology departments—if they tell you "facts" about history or interpretations of books that contradict everything you've learned, you're in trouble. To find out if you must be politically correct to attend a certain college, meet with members of the college's Young Republicans, or talk to parachurch groups like Campus Crusade. If the campus doesn't have such groups, you're in trouble.

Undoubtedly, all the knowledge you have gained by reading this book has made the college selection process seem a little more scary. Before you found out about all the problems with higher education, you may have even thought that most colleges were basically the same. Now you know that even schools that call themselves Christian can seriously undermine a student's faith, and that no college is totally "safe." Still, you may take comfort in one fact: properly prepared Christian students can attend college almost anywhere without that school adversely affecting their Christian commitment.

When it's all said and done, there are only two kinds of people in the world: those who build their lives on a sure foundation, and those who build their lives on shifting sand (Matthew 7:24-27). As Christians, we have the chance to build on the true foundation, provided we don't compromise its structure by mixing our Christianity with other worldviews or left-wing theories. Investing the time to ensure your foundation is uncompromised is the best investment you can make.

TWELVE

A CHAPTER JUST
FOR STUDENTS

As promised, it's time for the parents to leave the room. This chapter deals exclusively with questions and advice for you, the student.

We'll begin with two questions—one that you hear all the time, and one that is more important than any other question in the world. First, the most important one: Are you a Christian?

No one is a Christian just because his parents are, or because he goes to church. No one is a Christian just because he has gone through some religious ritual like baptism. We become Christians only when, first, we know that Jesus, the Son of God, died for our sins and rose from the dead as proof that all who believe in Him will also be delivered from death (see 1 Corinthians 15). Then we must act on that knowledge and accept Jesus as our Savior and Lord (see Romans 10:9-10).

Nothing you do will ever reconcile you with God.

The only way to be saved is to completely rely on God's grace—that is, to trust Christ to do what you cannot do. If you're not certain about your relationship with Jesus, talk about it with someone.

The second question—brace yourself—is the same question you hear from your high school guidance counselor and Aunt Gertie and just about everyone else you know: What do you want to do with your life? The Bible teaches that the life of a Christian is not his own. We have been bought with a price; thus, our life belongs to the One who redeemed us (see 1 Corinthians 6:20 and Romans 12:1-2). If you want your life to count for God, then your choice of a college must be seen in the light of your total commitment to His will. Perhaps God wants you to serve Him in some type of full-time Christian service; perhaps He wants you to serve Him in the business world or as a computer programmer or a teacher. Don't think of college as a means to achieve selfish goals; instead, see it as a necessary step in preparing for the life-work that God wants you to perform. Keep God's will and His call before you as you make your decision.

Ten Pieces of Advice

The previous two chapters helped you prepare for some of the intellectual challenges you'll face at college; the following advice will prepare you to thrive physically, mentally, *and* spiritually. You can always choose to ignore this advice today—but eventually you'll learn it anyway, from a much more cruel teacher: experience.

1) Don't keep your problems and difficulties to

yourself. Lots of people are in a position to help and want to be of assistance—but they can't help if they don't know you're in trouble! If you run into questions you can't answer, the worst mistake you can make is to assume that there are no answers. Nothing you encounter at college is really new; other people have been down the same road before you, have confronted the same challenges, and have won. Somewhere the answer you're seeking and the help you need is available. Talk to people—including people at ministries like the Summit or Focus on the Family—and read good books like those listed in our bibliography.

2) Don't be a loner. No Christian has to feel isolated at *any* college. You can find believers to fellowship with anywhere, by taking a few simple steps. First, attend Bible-believing churches in your new community. Don't just visit as a stranger on Sunday morning—attend the Sunday school class for people your age, and really get involved. If the first church you attend doesn't have what you're seeking, keep looking. When you find a suitable church home, make an appointment with the pastor. Ask if he can provide information about local Christian organizations like Campus Crusade or the Navigators. Then get involved with these organizations.

Go the extra mile to build lasting Christian friendships. Your effort will pay huge dividends in times of trouble. "Two are better than one, because they have a good return for their work: If one falls down, his friend can help him up. But pity the man who falls and has no one to help him up! . . . A cord of three strands is not quickly broken" (Ecclesiastes 4:9-10,12b).

3) Be careful about the company you keep. The Apostle Paul gave some good advice on this matter: "Do not be misled. Bad company corrupts good character" (1 Corinthians 15:33). No matter where you attend college, you'll have choices to make about your companions. Don't gravitate in the direction of people whose conduct and character are questionable. To take captive every thought for Christ, surround yourself with friends striving to do the same.

4) Be alert to challenges to your faith from teachers and students. Christ tells us that those who are ashamed of Him now will find Him ashamed of them on the Day of Judgment (Mark 8:38). What's more, defending your faith at college will provide a powerful testimony to people who may have previously assumed that Christianity was irrational. Standing up for your convictions may eventually lead others to embrace those convictions.

5) Be faithful in your private devotions. Don't think that spending time with God is somehow beneath you now that you've reached the exalted status of college student. Read God's Word and talk to Him! Commitment to a quiet time will accomplish at least three things: God will hear you (James 5:15-16), you will hear from God (Matthew 7:7-8), and you will grow in righteousness (2 Timothy 3:16-17).[1]

6) Watch for cults. We've already warned you about Mormons, Jehovah's Witnesses, Christian Scientists, and Moonies, but these "high profile" cults are only the tip of the iceberg. Don't believe everything an organization says just because it calls itself Christian. Compare everything they teach with the Word of God. If they contradict scripture, avoid them like the plague.[2]

7) Watch for special teachers on your campus. Even an absolutely horrendous school like the University of Colorado features a few candles in the darkness. When you find a teacher that really loves his discipline and has a knack for communicating this love, take as many courses taught by him as possible. After all, you don't just walk into a library and check books out at random—you attempt to find authors who communicate truth well. In the same way, don't take classes at random. This is another means of maximizing your educational dollar.

8) Watch for professors who share your faith. At Ron's old university, for example, about forty Christian professors regularly place an ad in the student newspaper. The ad lists their names and departments, identifies them as Christians, and invites interested students to visit them. If you have a chance, try to take courses from such people; get to know them personally. In some cases, you may make a friend for life.

9) If you make a mistake and get in a bad class, it may be best to drop the course (just make sure you don't miss the withdrawal deadline and get a failing grade). As soon as you sense you're going to have problems with a teacher, see if you can take the same course from a different teacher. Even if you can't take the course from another teacher, it might still be wisest to drop the course and try to pick it up in summer school or at another college. You need never feel guilty about dropping a course taught by someone more interested in indoctrination than teaching—this professor is basically stealing the money you meant to spend on an education.

On the other hand, don't begin dropping classes at

the drop of a hat, for frivolous reasons like the professor's hairstyle. Quitting anything is a serious decision, because quitting can become addictive: the more you quit, the easier it gets to quit again. When considering dropping a class, pray about it and consult your family—then trust God to lead you according to His will.

10) If you discover that you've picked the wrong college, it's best to transfer to a different school rather than languishing in the wrong environment for four long years. But once again, pay attention to the rules of the college. It is certainly better to complete a semester, earn your credits, and transfer them to a new school than to drop out in the middle of a semester and lose all the work, time, and money you've already invested. Every year, we see students leave school without going through the proper withdrawal procedures. These students end up with automatic "F"s for all their courses, so that whenever they transfer, those "F"s follow them like Mary's little lamb.

Real Wisdom

Enough advice from us. Turn now to the ultimate Advisor and the Fount of all wisdom. What does He have to say about your college experience?

> Therefore everyone who hears these words of mine and puts them into practice is like a wise man who built his house on the rock. The rain came down, the streams rose, and the winds blew and beat against that house;

yet it did not fall, because it had its foundation
on the rock. But everyone who hears these
words of mine and does not put them into
practice is like a foolish man who built his
house on sand. The rain came down, the
streams rose, and the winds blew and beat
against that house, and it fell with a great
crash. (Matthew 7:24-27)

Lots of kids go off to college with high hopes and
then mess up their lives with immorality and drugs. Lots of
kids who call themselves Christians turn away from Christ at
school. Why? Because their lives were built on shifting sand.
The apostle Paul tells us that the sure foundation is Jesus
Christ (1 Corinthians 3:11). People whose lives are built on
this foundation are better able to withstand whatever storms
savage their lives.

First Peter 5:8 also contains some good advice: "Be
self-controlled and alert. Your enemy the devil prowls
around like a roaring lion looking for someone to devour.
Resist him, standing firm in the faith . . ." Don't think of
college as a vacation; think of it as an adventure. As a
Christian, you'll step on most campuses with a target on your
forehead, as a member of the only group that it's politically
correct to belittle. "The last respectable bigotry in the United
States" says Michael Novak, "is against evangelicals and
fundamentalists. It seems perfectly acceptable to utter
insulting language about them amongst people who would be
ashamed of uttering the same sort of language about anybody
else."[3] Your mind will be tested; your faith will be tested;

your character will be tested. Approach these tests
determined to persevere in Christ.

Ephesians 6:10-18 tells college students—and every
Christian—what preparations they must make to ensure that
they will persevere:

> Finally, be strong in the Lord and in his
> mighty power. Put on the full armor of God
> so that you can take your stand against the
> devil's schemes. For our struggle is not
> against flesh and blood, but against the rulers,
> against the authorities, against the powers of
> this dark world and against the spiritual
> forces of evil in the heavenly realms.
> Therefore put on the full armor of God, so
> that when the day of evil comes, you may be
> able to stand your ground, and after you have
> done everything, to stand. Stand firm then,
> with the belt of truth buckled around your
> waist, with the breastplate of righteousness in
> place, and with your feet fitted with the
> readiness that comes from the gospel of
> peace. In addition to all this, take up the shield
> of faith, with which you can extinguish all the
> flaming arrows of the evil one. Take the
> helmet of salvation and the sword of the
> Spirit, which is the word of God. And pray in

the Spirit on all occasions with all kinds of prayers and requests.

The wisdom contained in this passage merits another book in itself. Consider just the following points: (1) You are part of a conflict that is often not visible to the human eye. (2) God has provided everything you'll need to come through this struggle successfully. (3) In order to persevere, you must put on the armor that God has provided. (4) Be sure to stand firm; compromising with lies and sinful actions leads to defeat. (5) You don't have to be afraid of any truth in any field since God Himself is the Author of all truth. Don't think that you have to run from science or philosophy or anything else in order to protect your faith. All truth is God's truth. (6) Remember the breastplate of righteousness. The battle ahead of you is not only an intellectual one; to survive the conflict you must live a life of integrity and selflessness. (7) Confidence in the gospel gives us ability to act and move. (8) Your faith in Christ is a shield that can protect you from whatever arrows are shot in your direction. (9) The helmet of salvation is an important part of your armor. If you have doubts about your salvation, your enemy will exploit the openings that these doubts give him. (10) Never ignore the sword of the Spirit. Study God's inspired Word. Let the truth of that Word give you guidance, encouragement, and wisdom. (11) Finally, pray in the Spirit. Keep your lines of communication with God open. Share your fears and needs with Him on a regular basis, and let Him demonstrate His power as He answers your prayers.

Conclusion

As you put on the full armor of God, notice that you must begin with *truth*. There is no substitute for the acquisition of knowledge and wisdom; there is no substitute for hard work and hard study. Christians, more than anyone else, should be thrilled at the opportunity to attend college, because college allows students to focus on the pursuit of truth.

Unfortunately, too many Christians buy into the lie that the pursuit of knowledge is somehow incompatible with the life of the righteous man. Such Christians worship a small God who bears very little resemblance to the God of all wisdom and knowledge (Colossians 2:2-3). True pursuit of the true God involves the pursuit of truth.

Of course, it is possible to love knowledge too dearly, placing your zeal for knowledge above your zeal for God. This perspective is also a desperate mistake. Knowledge without love—for God and for our neighbors—just puffs us up (1 Corinthians 8:1). We should never seek knowledge for its own sake; we should seek knowledge because it pleases God.

Today, you are prepared to choose a college that will help you pursue truth while focusing on Christ. As you step on campus to begin this pursuit, you will also begin building a house. The true foundation, Jesus Christ, will guarantee that your house—your life and your work—will stand. But be careful about the materials you use to build on this foundation. "If any man builds on this foundation using gold, silver, costly stones, wood, hay or straw, his work will be shown for what it is, because the Day will bring it to light. It will be revealed with fire, and the fire will test the quality of each man's work. If what he has built survives, he will receive his reward" (1 Corinthians 3:12-14). Take care that the life you build is not carelessly thrown together or made of shoddy parts. In college and beyond, see to it that your house will survive the fire.

NOTES

Chapter Two

1. For a more complete discussion of evangelicalism, see Ronald Nash, *Evangelicalism in America* (Nashville, TN: Abingdon Press, 1987). To understand how evangelicals relate to America's liberal "mainline denominations," see Ronald Nash, ed., *Evangelical Renewal in the Mainline Churches* (Westchester, IL: Crossway Books, 1987).

2. James Orr, *The Christian View of God and the World* (New York, NY: Scribner, 1904), p. 20.

3. Ibid.

4. Ibid, pp. 20-21.

5. Allan Bloom, *The Closing of the American Mind* (Chicago, IL: University of Chicago Press, 1987), p. 57.

6. Ibid., p. 58.

7. Ibid., p. 64.

8. Ibid.

Chapter Three

1. Gary Lyle Railsback, "An Exploratory Study of the Religiosity and Related Outcomes Among College Students" (PhD diss., University of California Los Angeles, 1994), pp. 59-60.

2. One terrific way to prepare yourself for college is to participate in a Summit Ministries two-week Christian Leadership Seminar. These college prep seminars can be taken for college credit, and provide an important insight into the ideologies that conflict on college campuses. These seminars are highly recommended by Christian leaders like Dr. James Dobson, Dr. D. James Kennedy, and Dr. J.P. Moreland.

Chapter Four

1. Students who score in the top one-half of one percent for their state on the PSAT become National Merit semi-finalists. National Merit Scholarships range from one-time awards of $1,000 to annual awards of $1,500 for up to four years. For more information, write to the National Merit Scholarship Program, 990 Grove Street, Evanston, IL 60201.

2. Other kinds of tests help you determine your interests and personality type. Don't feel that you must rely solely on aptitude tests—certain personality tests like the Meyers-Briggs Personality Inventory can also help you determine your college major.

3. The PCG test is published by CTB/Macmillan/McGraw-Hill, and the Strong Interest Inventory is published by Stanford University Press.

Chapter Five

1. Thomas Sowell, *Choosing a College* (New York: Harper and Row, 1989), p. 108.

2. Ibid., p. 78.

3. Charles J. Sykes and Brand Miner, *The National Review College Guide* (New York: Harper and Row, 1993), p. 242.

Chapter Six

1. For examples of such courses, see Martin Anderson, *Impostors in the Temple* (New York, NY: Simon and Schuster, 1992).

Chapter Seven

1. Kalman A. Chany and Geoff Martz, *The Student Access Guide to Paying for College* (New York, NY: Villard, 1992), pp. 20-21.

2. Marguerite J. Dennis, *Keys to Financing a College Education* (New York, NY: Barron's, 1993), p. 6.

3. George Roche, "How Government Funding is Destroying American Higher Education," *Imprimis*, October 1994, p. 3.

4. George Roche, *The Fall of the Ivory Tower* (Washington, DC: Regnery Publishing, 1994), p. 211.

5. Roche, "How Government Funding is Destroying American Higher Education," p. 4.

6. For more information about this program, write: National

Commission for Cooperative Education, 360 Huntington Avenue, Boston, MA 02215.

Chapter Eight

1. Christian College Coalition, *Consider a Christian College* (Princeton, NJ: Peterson's Guides, 1988), p. 11.

2. One example of a large public university that avoids most of these problems is Texas A&M. Not only does this school generally provide a good educational value—it also boasts a faculty that includes more than 150 committed Christians.

3. James Davison Hunter, *Evangelicalism, The Coming Generation* (Chicago: University of Chicago Press, 1987), p. 178.

Chapter Nine

1. Carl F.H. Henry, *Evangelicals in Search of Identity* (Waco, TX: Word Books, 1976), p. 42.

2. Richard Quebedeaux, *The Worldly Evangelicals* (San Francisco, CA: Harper and Row, 1978), p. 93. The fact that Quebedeaux's book was published almost 20 years ago should not create false hope that things have improved. If anything, they have deteriorated.

3. Ibid.

4. Ibid.

5. To protect this student's privacy, we use a fictitious name.

6. Don Feder, "What Does the Radical Left Want on Campus?" *Human Events*, March 12, 1988, p. 240.

7. The meaning of political correctness is discussed in a later chapter.

8. For the record, Southern Baptist colleges remain, by and large, rather liberal institutions. This is due to the fact that the denomination's colleges are controlled by state conventions instead of the more conservative national convention.

Chapter Ten

1. A more technical definition of the term "worldview" is provided by David A. Noebel in the must-read worldview text *Understanding the Times: The Religious Worldviews of Our Day and the Search for Truth* (Eugene, OR: Harvest House, 1991). Noebel says

a worldview is "any ideology, philosophy, theology, movement, or religion that provides an overarching approach to understanding God, the world, and man's relation to God and the world" (p. 8). Students will also benefit from reading Ronald Nash, *Worldviews in Conflict* (Grand Rapids, MI: Zondervan Publishing, 1992).

2. *Humanist Manifestoes I & II* (Buffalo, NY: Prometheus Books, 1973), pp. 7-10.

3. For a detailed discussion of Marxism/Leninism, see Noebel, *Understanding the Times*.

4. M. Russell Ballard, *Our Search for Happiness* (Salt Lake City, UT: Deseret Book Co., 1993), p. 87.

5. Kevin Bywater, "The Marks of the Cults" (Manitou Springs, CO: Mind Renewal, 1995). Mind Renewal Books and Communications can be contacted by writing P.O. Box 162, Manitou Springs, CO 80829.

6. See George Marsden, *The Soul of the American University* (New York, NY: Oxford University Press, 1994).

7. See Ronald Nash, *Christian Faith and Historical Understanding* (Richardson, TX: Probe Books, 1992).

8. James Davison Hunter, *Evangelicals, The Coming Generation* (Chicago, IL: University of Chicago Press, 1987), p. 26.

9. See Ronald Nash, *The Closing of the American Heart: What's Really Wrong with America's Schools* (Richardson, TX: Probe Books, 1990), Humberto Belli and Ronald Nash, *Beyond Liberation Theology* (Grand Rapids, MI: Baker Book House, 1992), and Emilio Nunez, *Liberation Theology* (Chicago, IL: Moody Press, 1985).

10. Apologetics refers to the philosophical defense of the Christian faith. For an introduction to apologetics, read C.S. Lewis, *Mere Christianity* (New York, NY: Macmillan, 1952).

Chapter Eleven

1. Paul Hollander, *The Survival of the Adversary Culture* (New Brunswick, NJ: Transaction Books, 1988), p. 14.

2. William E. Simon, "To Reopen the American Mind," *The Wall Street Journal*, July 8, 1988.

3. Ibid.

4. Georgie Anne Geyer, "Marxism Thrives on Campus," *The Denver Post*, August 29, 1989, p. B7.

5. David B. Richardson, "Marxism in U.S. Classrooms," *U.S.*

News and World Report, January 25, 1982, pp. 42-45.

6. Geyer, "Marxism Thrives on Campus," p. B7.

1. Ibid.

8. For a more detailed description of neo-Marxism, see Ronald Nash, *Poverty and Wealth* (Richardson, TX: Probe Books, 1992).

9. See Anthony Campolo, *We Have Met the Enemy, and They Are Partly Right* (Waco, TX: Word Books, 1985), chapters 7-9.

10. Lee Congdon, "The Marxist Chameleon," *The Intercollegiate Review*, Fall 1987, p. 17.

11. Christina Hoff Sommers, "Feminism and the College Curriculum," *Imprimis*, June 1990, p. 4.

12. *Syracuse University Magazine*, December, 1990, pp. 44-45.

13. Ibid.

14. For the whole story, see Dinesh D'Souza, *Illiberal Education: The Politics of Race and Sex on Campus* (New York, NY: Macmillan, 1991), pp. 202-203.

15. This sounds like a joke, but it's not. According to "Students at CU study bare facts in Madonna video," *Colorado Springs Gazette-Telegraph*, July 7, 1993, p. B3, University of Colorado students could enroll in a course entitled "Studies in Gender and Performance: Madonna Undressed." The course included a viewing of Madonna's pornographic video "Erotica," which was even too lewd for MTV.

Chapter Twelve

1. If you haven't yet committed to spending about 20 minutes in prayer and Bible study each day, and don't know how to start, try reading J.I. Packer, *Knowing God* (Downers Grove, IL: InterVarsity Press, 1993). Read four or five pages in this classic each morning, look up the scripture references mentioned in those pages, and then spend some time talking to God about what you're learning and how it applies to your life.

2. For more information on cults, see Ronald Enroth, et al. *A Guide to Cults and New Religions* (Downers Grove, IL: InterVarsity Press, 1983).

3. Michael Cromartie interviewing Michael Novak, "The Good Capitalist," *Christianity Today*, October 24, 1994, p. 31.

TOPICAL BIBLIOGRAPHY

APOLOGETICS

Chesterton, G.K. *Orthodoxy*. Wheaton, IL: Harold Shaw Publishers, 1994.

Clark, Kelly James. *Return to Reason*. Grand Rapids, MI: Eerdmans Publishing, 1990.

Craig, William Lane. *Reasonable Faith: Christian Truth and Apologetics*. Westchester, IL: Crossway Books, 1994.

Joad, C.E.M. *The Recovery of Belief.* London: Faber and Faber Limited, 1955. Out of print.

Lewis, C.S. *Mere Christianity*. New York, NY: Macmillan, 1952.

Lewis, C.S. *Miracles*. New York, NY: Macmillan, 1947.

Lewis, C.S. *The Problem of Pain*. New York, NY: Macmillan, 1962.

Moreland, J.P. *Scaling the Secular City*. Grand Rapids, MI: Baker Book House, 1987.

Nash, Ronald. *Faith and Reason: Searching for a Rational Faith*. Grand Rapids, MI: Zondervan Publishing, 1988.

BIBLICAL CRITICISM

Blomberg, Craig L. *The Historical Reliability of the Gospels*. Downers Grove, IL: InterVarsity Press, 1987.

Bruce, F.F. *New Testament Documents: Are They Reliable?*

Downers Grove, IL: InterVarsity Press, 1967.

Carson, D.A., and John D. Woodbridge, eds. *Scripture and Truth*. Grand Rapids, MI: Baker Book House, 1992.

Harrison, R.K. *Biblical Criticism: Historical, Literary, and Textual*. Grand Rapids, MI: Zondervan Publishing, 1978.

Linnemann, Eta. *Historical Criticism of the Bible: Methodology or Ideology?* Grand Rapids, MI: Baker Book House, 1990.

Nash, Ronald. *Christian Faith and Historical Understanding*. Dallas, TX: Probe Books, 1989.

CHRISTIANITY

Bruce, F.F. *Jesus: Lord and Savior*. Downers Grove, IL: InterVarsity Press, 1986.

Bruce, F.F. *Know the Truth: A Handbook of Christian Belief*. Downers Grove, IL: InterVarsity Press, 1982. Out of print.

Colson, Charles. *Loving God*. Grand Rapids, MI: Zondervan Publishing, 1987.

Henry, Carl F.H. *God, Revelation and Authority*. Six volumes. Waco, TX: Word Publishing, 1983. Out of print.

Kennedy, D. James, and Jerry Newcombe. *What if Jesus Had Never Been Born?* Nashville, TN: Thomas Nelson Publishers, 1994.

Kreeft, Peter. *Three Philosophies of Life*. San Francisco, CA: Ignatius Press, 1989.

Packer, J.I. *Knowing God*. Downers Grove, IL: InterVarsity Press, 1993.

Schaeffer, Francis A. *A Christian Manifesto*. Westchester, IL: Crossway Books, 1981.

Schaeffer, Francis A. *How Should We Then Live?* Westchester, IL: Crossway Books, 1983.

Stott, John. *Basic Christianity.* Downers Grove, IL: InterVarsity Press, 1964.

CULTS

Enroth, Ronald, et al. *A Guide to Cults and New Religions.* Downers Grove, IL: InterVarsity Press, 1983.

Grass, Edmond C. *Cults and the Occult.* Phillipsburg, NJ: Presbyterian and Reformed, 1994.

Martin, Walter. *The Kingdom of the Cults.* Minneapolis, MN: Bethany House Publishers, 1985.

Rhodes, Ron. *The Culting of America: The Shocking Implications for Every Concerned Christian.* Eugene, OR: Harvest House, 1994.

Sire, James W. *Scripture Twisting: Twenty Ways the Cults Misread the Bible.* Downers Grove, IL: InterVarsity Press, 1980.

CULTURE

Beisner, E. Calvin. *Prosperity and Poverty.* Westchester, IL: Crossway Books, 1988.

Gilder, George. *Men and Marriage.* Gretna, LA: Pelican Publishing, 1986.

Kilpatrick, William. *Why Johnny Can't Tell Right from Wrong.* New York, NY: Simon and Schuster, 1992.

Lewis, C.S. *The Abolition of Man.* New York, NY: Macmillan, 1978.

Marsden, George M. *The Soul of the American University: From Protestant Establishment to Established Nonbelief.* New York, NY: Oxford University Press, 1994.

Medved, Michael. *Hollywood vs. America: Popular Culture and the War on Traditional Values.* New York, NY:

HarperCollins Publishers, 1992.

Nash, Ronald. *Closing of the American Heart: What's Really Wrong with America's Schools.* Dallas, TX: Probe Books, 1990.

Olasky, Marvin. *The Tragedy of American Compassion.* Washington, DC: Regnery Gateway, 1992.

Schlossberg, Herbert. *Idols for Destruction: The Conflict of Christian Faith and American Culture.* Westchester, IL: Crossway Books, 1993.

Veith, Gene Edward. *State of the Arts.* Westchester, IL: Crossway Books, 1991.

Wood, Glenn G., and John E. Dietrich. *The AIDS Epidemic: Balancing Compassion and Justice.* Portland, OR: Multnomah Press, 1990. Out of print.

Marxism/Leninism and Secular Humanism

Bockmuehl, Klaus. *The Challenge of Marxism.* Colorado Springs, CO: Holmers and Howard, 1988. Out of print.

Kurtz, Paul, ed. *Humanist Manifestoes I & II.* Buffalo, NY: Prometheus Books, 1973.

Marx, Karl. *The Communist Manifesto.* New York, NY: Bantam Books, 1992.

Nash, Ronald. *Poverty and Wealth: Why Socialism Doesn't Work.* Dallas, TX: Probe Books, 1992.

Noebel, David A., J.F. Baldwin, and Kevin Bywater, eds. *Clergy in the Classroom: The Religion of Secular Humanism.* Manitou Springs, CO: Summit Press, 1995.

Solzhenitsyn, Alexander I. *The Gulag Archipelago.* New York, NY: HarperCollins Publishers, 1991.

Van der Heydt, Barbara. *Candles Behind the Wall.* Grand Rapids, MI: Eerdmans Publishing, 1993.

Albrecht, Mark. *Reincarnation: A Christian Critique of a New Age Doctrine.* Downers Grove, IL: InterVarsity Press, 1987.

Anderson, Norman. *Christianity and World Religions.* Downers Grove, IL: InterVarsity Press, 1984.

Ankerberg, John, and Craig Branch. *Thieves of Innocence.* Eugene, OR: Harvest House, 1993.

Clark, David K., and Norman L. Geisler. *Apologetics in the New Age: A Christian Critique of Pantheism.* Grand Rapids, MI: Baker Book House, 1990.

Groothuis, Douglas. *Confronting the New Age.* Downers Grove, IL: InterVarsity Press, 1988.

Groothuis, Douglas. *Revealing the New Age Jesus.* Downers Grove, IL: InterVarsity Press, 1990.

Groothuis, Douglas. *Unmasking the New Age.* Downers Grove, IL: InterVarsity Press, 1986.

Mangalwadi, Vishal. *When the New Age Gets Old.* Downers Grove, IL: InterVarsity Press, 1992.

POLITICS

Amos, Gary T. *Defending the Declaration.* Brentwood, TN: Wolgemuth and Hyatt, 1989. Out of print.

Bastiat, Frederic. *The Law.* Irvington-on-Hudson, NY: The Foundation for Economic Education, 1990.

Colson, Charles. *Kingdoms in Conflict.* Grand Rapids, MI: Zondervan Publishing, 1987.

Henry, Carl F.H. *Twilight of a Great Civilization.* Westchester, IL: Crossway Books, 1988.

Kirk, Russell. *The Politics of Prudence.* Bryn Mawr, PA: Intercollegiate Studies Institute, 1993.

Kirk, Russell. *The Roots of American Order*. Washington, DC: Regnery Gateway, 1992.

Nash, Ronald. *Freedom, Justice and the State*. Lanham, MD: University Press of America, 1980.

Whitehead, John W. *The Second American Revolution*. Westchester, IL: Crossway Books, 1988.

THE RADICAL AGENDA

Bernstein, Richard. *Dictatorship of Virtue: Multiculturalism and the Battle for America's Future*. New York, NY: Alfred A. Knopf, 1994.

D'Souza, Dinesh. *Illiberal Education: The Politics of Race and Sex on Campus*. New York, NY: Macmillan, 1991.

Kimball, Roger. *Tenured Radicals: How Politics Has Corrupted our Higher Education*. New York, NY: Harper and Row, 1991.

SCIENCE AND THE EVOLUTION DEBATE

Davis, Percival, and Dean H. Kenyon. *Of Pandas and People*. Dallas, TX: Haughton Publishing, 1989.

Hummel, Charles. *The Galileo Connection*. Downers Grove, IL: InterVarsity Press, 1986.

Jaki, Stanley L. *The Savior of Science*. Washington, DC: Regnery Gateway, 1988. Out of print.

Johnson, Philip E. *Darwin on Trial*. Downers Grove, IL: InterVarsity Press, 1991.

Moreland, J.P. *Christianity and the Nature of Science*. Grand Rapids, MI: Baker Book House, 1989.

Moreland, J.P., ed. *The Creation Hypothesis: Scientific Evidence for an Intelligent Designer*. Downers Grove, IL: InterVarsity Press, 1994.

Morris, Henry M. *The Long War Against God.* Grand Rapids, MI: Baker Book House, 1989.

Pearcey, Nancy R., and Charles B. Thaxton. *The Soul of Science: Christian Faith and Natural Philosophy.* Wheaton, IL: Crossway Books, 1994.

Taylor, Ian T. *In the Minds of Men: Darwin and the New World Order.* Toronto, Canada: TFE Publishing, 1991.

THEOLOGICAL LIBERALISM

Belli, Humberto, and Ronald Nash. *Beyond Liberation Theology.* Grand Rapids, MI: Baker Book House, 1992.

Craig, William Lane. *Knowing the Truth About the Resurrection.* Ann Arbor, MI: Servant Books, 1988.

Green, Michael. *The Empty Cross of Jesus.* Downers Grove, IL: InterVarsity Press, 1984. Out of print.

Habermas, Gary. *The Resurrection of Jesus: An Apologetic.* Grand Rapids, MI: Baker Book House, 1980. Out of print.

Nash, Ronald. *The Concept of God.* Grand Rapids, MI: Zondervan Publishing, 1983.

Nash, Ronald. *Is Jesus the Only Savior?* Grand Rapids, MI: Zondervan Publishing, 1994.

Nash, Ronald, ed. *Liberation Theology.* Grand Rapids, MI: Baker Book House, 1988.

Nash, Ronald, ed. *Process Theology.* Grand Rapids, MI: Baker Book House, 1987. Out of print.

Nash, Ronald. *Social Justice and the Christian Church.* Grand Rapids, MI: Baker Book House, 1987.

Nash, Ronald. *The Word of God and the Mind of Man.* Phillipsburg, NJ: Presbyterian and Reformed, 1992.

Breese, David A. *Seven Men Who Rule the World from the Grave.* Chicago, IL: Moody Press, 1990.

Brown, William E., and W. Gary Phillips. *Making Sense of Your World.* Chicago, IL: Moody Press, 1991.

Clark, Gordon. *Thales to Dewey.* Jefferson, MD: The Trinity Foundation, 1985.

Dobson, James C., and Gary L. Bauer. *Children at Risk: The Battle for the Hearts and Minds of our Kids.* Dallas, TX: Word Publishing, 1992.

Evans, C. Stephen. *Philosophy of Religion: Thinking About Faith.* Downers Grove, IL: InterVarsity Press, 1985.

Nash, Ronald. *Worldviews in Conflict.* Grand Rapids, MI: Zondervan Publishers, 1992.

Neill, Stephen. *Christian Faith and Other Faiths.* Downers Grove, IL: InterVarsity Press, 1984.

Noebel, David A. *Understanding the Times: The Religious Worldviews of Our Day and the Search for Truth.* Eugene, OR: Harvest House, 1994. Unabridged.

Noebel, David A. *Understanding the Times: The Religious Worldviews of Our Day and the Search for Truth.* Manitou Springs, CO: ACSI and Summit Press, 1995. Abridged.

Roche, George. *A World Without Heroes.* Hillsdale, MI: Hillsdale College Press, 1987.

Sire, James W. *The Universe Next Door.* Downers Grove, IL: InterVarsity Press, 1988.

PERIODICALS WORTH READING

No matter what college you attend, students and professors at that school will get the bulk of their news from (usually liberal) daily newspapers and (almost always liberal) news magazines like *Newsweek* or *Time*. For a more accurate angle on the news, Christians need to rely on more trustworthy publications, like the following:

American Spectator (monthly news magazine). 2020 N. 14th St., Suite 750, Arlington, VA 22216. (703) 243-3733.

Christian Research Journal (scholarly quarterly that focuses on apologetics). Christian Research Institute, P.O. Box 500, San Juan Capistrano, CA 92693. (714) 855-9926.

Citizen (monthly family news update). Focus on the Family, 8605 Explorer Dr., Colorado Springs, CO 80920. (800) 232-6459.

Crisis (conservative Roman Catholic monthly magazine that focuses on campus issues like political correctness). P.O. Box 1006, Notre Dame, IN 46556. (219) 234-3759.

Commentary (conservative Jewish monthly news magazine). 165 E. 56th St., New York, NY 10022. (212) 751-4000.

First Things (Christian monthly magazine featuring news and scholarly essays). Department FT, P.O. Box 3000, Denville, NJ 07834. (800) 875-2997.

The Freeman (monthly magazine that focuses on political

and economic issues). Foundation for Economic Education, Irvington-on-Hudson, NY 10533. (914) 591-7230.

Imprimis (monthly transcript of a lecture by a nationally-known speaker). Hillsdale College, Hillsdale, MI 49242. (517) 437-7341.

The Journal (monthly compilation of news and essays from other sources). Summit Ministries, P.O. Box 207, Manitou Springs, CO 80829. (719) 685-9103.

National Review (bi-weekly news and opinion magazine). 150 E. 35th St., New York, NY 10016. (815) 734-1232.

Policy Review (quarterly magazine that focuses on foreign and domestic policies). Heritage Foundation, 214 Massachusetts Ave. NE, Washington, DC 20002. (202) 546-4400.

Washington Watch (monthly newsletter describing political issues that affect the family). Family Research Council, 700 13th St. NW, Washington, DC 20005. (202) 393-2100.

World (Christian news weekly that beats *Time* and *Newsweek* hands down). P.O. Box 2330, Asheville, NC 28802. (704) 253-8063.

ABOUT THE AUTHORS

Dr. Ronald Nash is professor of philosophy at Reformed Theological Seminary in Orlando, Florida. He previously served 27 years as head of the Department of Philosophy and Religion at Western Kentucky University. He received his PhD from Syracuse University. Ron is the author or editor of more than 25 books, including *Is Jesus the Only Savior?*, *Worldviews in Conflict*, *Great Divides*, and *The Closing of the American Heart*. He has lectured at more than 60 colleges and universities in the U.S. and spoken extensively in the former Soviet Union.

Jeff Baldwin is the Research Director for Summit Ministries. In this capacity, he served as the creative editor for David A. Noebel's worldview analysis text, *Understanding the Times* (now in its sixth printing), and the abridged version, which is featured in a Bible curriculum produced by ACSI. Jeff recently published his first novel, *Ian*, and his articles have appeared in *Teachers in Focus*, *The Teaching Home*, and *New Attitude*.

ABOUT SUMMIT MINISTRIES

Summit Ministries equips tomorrow's servant leaders to analyze competing worldviews and champion the Christian worldview, inspiring them to love God with their hearts, souls, minds and strength. This is accomplished through:

Understanding the Times: Both the abridged and unabridged versions compare and contrast the Christian worldview with the predominant false worldviews in Western civilization.

Understanding the Times Curriculum: With over 60 video segments and documentation, this curriculum provides all the information you need to teach your Christian high school or study group to understand the times and know what they ought to do (1 Chronicles 12:32).

Summer Christian Leadership Seminars: During these two-week academic camps, students 16 and older learn how to defend their faith and live for Christ.

The *Journal*: This monthly newsletter provides the best review of the news for Christians who don't have time to monitor all of the media.

Summit Bookhouse: Offers one of the best collections of thoughtful worldview-oriented books available in the Christian community.

For more information, call Summit Ministries at (719) 685-9103.